Run *Your* *Life* Like a Business

ONE STRATEGIC STEP AT A TIME

VALERIE PEARSON

Copyright © 2025 Valerie Pearson

ISBN: 978-0-9944780-9-2 eBook
ISBN: 978-0-9944780-8-5 Paperback

All rights reserved, including the right to reproduce this book or portions thereof in any form whatsoever. Apart from any fair dealing for the purpose of research, private study, criticism or review, no part of this publication may be reproduced, stored in or introduced into a retrieval system, or transmitted in any form or by any means (electronic, mechanical, photocopying, recording or otherwise), without the prior written permission of the copyright owner.

CONTENTS

Preface 1
My Story 7
Run Your Life Like a Business 17
Week One:
    The Daily Schedule 19
Week Two:
    Weekly, Monthly, and Yearly Schedules 31
Week Three:
    Medical and Dental Appointments 37
Week Four:
    Have a Home Office 39
Week Five:
    Journaling 41
Week Six:
    Make a Nighttime Ritual 47
Week Seven:
    Create a Habit Tracker 51
Week Eight:
    Exercise 55
Week Nine:
    Food and Mindful Meal Planning 61
Week Ten:
    Once-a-Week Meal Preparation 71
Week Eleven:
    Make a Food Budget 75
Week Twelve:
    Decluttering Your Home 79
Week Thirteen:
    Designing Your Personal Space 85
Week Fourteen:
    Goal Setting 87

Week Fifteen:
Creating a Vision Board 93
Week Sixteen:
Working Out Your Net Worth 97
Week Seventeen:
Creating Your Personal Income and Expenditure Statement 103
Week Eighteen:
Create a Budget 109
Week Nineteen:
High-Interest Accounts and No-Fee Credit Cards. 115
Week Twenty:
Get Paid What You Are Worth 119
Week Twenty-One:
Insurance. 127
Week Twenty-Two:
You and the Taxman 133
Week Twenty-Three:
Pay Yourself First 137
Week Twenty-Four:
Play the Frugal Game. 141
Week Twenty-Five:
Getting Out of Debt 145
Week Twenty-Six:
Avoid High-Cost, Low-Benefit Debt. 149
Week Twenty-Seven:
Owning Your Own Home 153
Week Twenty-Eight:
Investing for the Long Hall 159
Week Twenty-Nine:
Creating Passive Income 165
Week Thirty:
Meditation. 169
Week Thirty-One:
Be in the Now through Mindfulness. 171
Week Thirty-Two:
Connect with Nature 175

Week Thirty-Three:
   Create Your Personal Brand 177
Week Thirty-Four:
   Clothing 183
Week Thirty-Five:
   Reading for Self-Improvement 191
Week Thirty-Six:
   Education 195
Week Thirty-Seven:
   Having a Will 197
Week Thirty-Eight:
   Having a Family Trust 199
Week Thirty-Nine:
   Marriage 205
Week Forty:
   Children 213
Week Forty-One:
   Divorce Happens 217
Week Forty-Two:
   Having a Side Hustle or Starting Your Own Business 221
Week Forty-Three:
   Find a Mentor 229
Week Forty-Four:
   Productivity. 233
Week Forty-Five:
   Select Your Friends Carefully 237
Week Forty-Six:
   Social Credit through Helping Others 241
Week Forty-Seven:
   Social Saturday. 245
Week Forty-Eight:
   Self-Care Sunday 249
Week Forty-Nine:
   Having a Garden 253
Week Fifty:
   Having a Sustainable Home 257

Week Fifty-One:
    Travel. 261
Week Fifty-Two:
    Giving. 265
Where To From Here **269**
About the Author **271**
End Notes **273**

PREFACE

This book is about living a beautiful, simple, fantastic life. For me, this means a life rich with friends, family, culture, literature and art, good food, and good wine. It means the ability to travel or stay in your favourite place. It means a life without the stress of wondering how you will get by. It is a life where you are financially, physically, and emotionally self-sufficient. So, what does it mean to be self-sufficient?

To be financially self-sufficient, you would need more money coming in than money going out. It means having enough to meet your needs and then some. There may still be things you want to do or have that you can't afford, but you will be comfortable always having enough to cover the basics. You would never have to worry about how to pay the rent or your mortgage or how to pay for your car and its related expenses. The power bills, insurance, and other life costs would all be easily covered. You would have enough money for food, clothes, and medication.

Being financially self-sufficient is not the same as becoming a billionaire and having everything you ever dreamed of. You may still have to say no to some things, but only things you want, not things you need. For example, I would love to take a flight on SpaceX. The last time I checked, and yes, I checked, it would cost me over $400,000. I can safely say that I am financially self-sufficient without being able to afford a SpaceX flight.

To be physically self-sufficient, you must maintain your health to the best standard possible. We all have different bodies, genetics, and challenges, so this will look different for different people. But no matter what your starting point is, we can all eat healthily, get enough sleep, exercise, and not make big mistakes like smoking, drinking excessive alcohol, or taking recreational drugs. Some people might have an issue with this one, and that's OK. I don't want to take anything that will damage my body or something that could get me into legal trouble. You are just setting yourself up for a disaster.

Being emotionally self-sufficient means not needing anyone else to make you happy. Let me clarify this one. Humans are social creatures. We do well when we have meaningful connections, so having other people in our lives is more than OK. It's just not OK if your happiness depends on them. Yes, there are people in your life it would be devastating to lose. I adore my children and grandchildren, and I sure hope I don't outlive any of them. But the point is, I am happy with or without them. You need to be content and comfortable in your own company.

Unfortunately, many people, including a past version of myself, need others to make them feel fulfilled. These are the people looking for meaning in their lives through someone else. They can't be happy on their own. They tend to go from one relationship to another, trying to find happiness. When they are alone, they are lonely. When they are with other people, they are lonely. They are lonely because they are not good company for themselves. They feel isolated, with or without a lack of social contact. Being emotionally self-sufficient is being happy with people or when alone. Your emotional state is self-created, so you make yourself happy or unhappy. Making someone else responsible for your happiness is unfair to that person and yourself.

Only when you are emotionally self-sufficient can you truly love your own company and yourself. Once you have achieved this self-love, you will have better relationships with others. Being happy on your own doesn't mean you have to be on your own. It just means you *can* be. The power to be alone and not lonely is significant. I am pretty sure you won't settle for less than you deserve if being alone is quite OK with you. Then, when you do enter a relationship, it will be because this person makes you, an already happy person, even happier. This person will add to your already great life and not be expected to fill a void within yourself that only you can fill. It is not our partner's job to make us happy. Happiness is a state of mind, and that is our job.

Achieving this self-sufficient lifestyle takes a bit of work. It doesn't just happen. That should be obvious when looking around at all the stressed, overworked, unhappy, dependent people. But where do you start? What do you do first? To take your life from where it is now, to take control and run your life, instead of having it run you, you start by creating a plan. Things tend to get complicated if you don't have a plan. You don't know where you are or where you are going, so you get pushed along by life, and you end up in a complex mess of your own making and not where you expected to end up or where you want to be.

If you were going to build a house, you would have house plans, and you would need to submit these plans to the local council for approval. If you were going to start a business and went to the bank for funding, they would ask to see your business plan. You would follow a map or the GPS if travelling across the country. You stick to the path on a walking trail and not head off into the bush. I have done a fair bit of travelling, and I can tell you now that I always knew where I was and where I was going. Admittedly, there was a bit of adventure in between, and we can't plan for every eventuality. Nevertheless, we do need to have a plan.

Too many of us do not apply this basic logic to our lives. We wander through the years without a plan and then wonder how we got lost. That is just what I did. I ended up middle-aged, in financial and legal trouble, wondering how I could have been so stupid. How could I have let it all come to this?

I knew I was not stupid. I was educated, worked hard, had never been unemployed, always made good money, lived in nice houses, and had great kids. So, how could I have ended up in so much trouble? I got where I was because I had no plan. I just let things ride and hoped for the best. I can tell you now that it didn't work out well for me at all.

I am not telling you this because I want you to feel sorry for me. I am telling you this because I don't want what happened to me to happen to anyone else. I don't want it to happen to my children, grandchildren, friends, or associates. I don't want it to happen to you. In this book, I will tell you how I messed up my life by having no plan, taking no precautions, and not thinking about my future. I am sure many of you will see yourself in some of the things I have done.

PREFACE

After nearly losing everything, I picked myself up and did what I should have done long before: I created a plan—not just one big plan but many small projects within a bigger plan. I started planning everything in my life and found that planning makes things simple. Life became less complex and less stressful, and things became easy. Step by step, I planned out my life, taking baby steps at first until I was tackling the big things like getting the house of my dreams and building an investment portfolio.

I didn't start with the big-ticket items. I started with the small plans to get me through the day and then through the week. Does that sound too small? We need these small plans when things aren't going well or we know they could improve. These small daily and weekly plans significantly impact monthly and yearly goals. After nearly losing everything, not once but twice, these small plans were all I could handle, and they made a big difference to the quality of my daily life and my mental well-being.

I will share plans you can make and execute to get where you want to go. I'll start with simple daily and weekly rituals you can adopt, all the way to relaxing on a mountain top or a beach if that's your thing, knowing you have a secure future and can handle anything that comes your way.

This is not a quick fix but a way of life. I'd recommend that you don't just read this book and put it on the shelf. Start at the beginning and follow the path, step by step, to the end. Some of you may have already mastered a step or two. That's great. If you already have a few steps in the bag, then so much the better for you. We are all in different places, so if you have meal planning for health and wealth sorted, read through that section to see if you can pick up any tips and then move on to the next area.

Some of what I cover could be called common sense, stuff we should already know. What surprised me the most was that my mistakes seem ridiculous when I look back, but I didn't know then what I know now. I spent a lot of time wondering why no one had taught me this stuff. They don't teach these life skills in school, nor at home most of the time either.I am writing this book for my children and grandchildren, for you and your sons and daughters. Let's hope they never have to say, Why didn't anyone teach me this stuff?

How did I mess up my life?

To understand where I am coming from and why I plan my life the way I do, you need to know where I have been. My experiences have given me some points of view that you may disagree with. I have formed some controversial perspectives on the structure of society, as the society we live in forms the basis of the rules by which we play this game called life. Please read with an open mind and see if you can imagine a more equitable social structure. Understanding the one we have and its rules is a great start.

MY STORY

I was born in England, but my family immigrated to Australia when I was only five. My childhood memories are of growing up in Queensland, Australia. I lived in a very traditional household. Mom stayed home and looked after the house and garden, while Dad went to work and brought the paycheque home. We lived in a lovely suburb in a three-bedroom home. I had a big brother and a dog. I don't think you could get more traditional if you tried.

Mom managed the household finances, like shopping and paying the bills, but you knew that Dad was the money maker and, ultimately, the boss. I loved my dad very much and only have good memories of him as a dad, and I also thought my parents got on great. I don't ever remember them even arguing. Looking back at my childhood through adult eyes, Mom and Dad could not have been as perfect as I remember, but they must have been pretty good. When I think of my childhood, I believe I was truly blessed. I did not even know child abuse or extreme poverty existed. I knew people were suffering in other parts of the world, but things in Australia looked pretty rosy. I was sheltered within my loving family.

I left school and got a job. I had no plan, was not interested in further education, and just wanted to have fun, travel, and go with the flow.

When I was twenty-one, I moved to America on a three-year working visa. I didn't have a plan; I just wanted to see the world. I saw many places in America and spent several months in Mexico. I popped in and out of America, extending my visa, without considering what I would do next. Again, there was no plan.

When I was twenty-five, I met someone who I thought was terrific, and it wasn't too long before we were married. My new husband and I moved to Louisiana, then to Texas, then to Pennsylvania, and finally ended up in Georgia. By the time we arrived in Georgia, I had three children. And, no, I did not plan that part of my life either. I was, however, thrilled with the size of my family, so that is one area where planning, or the lack thereof, was not an issue. This was more good luck than anything else, so I can't take any credit for planning the perfect number of children.

I thought we had finally found our forever home in Georgia. We bought some land and built a house. I remember the day we went to the solicitor's office to sign all the papers for the purchase of the land, the documents relating to the building package, and the home loan to go with all of this. I took time off work and met my husband there. We went into the office and went over the paperwork. That is when I discovered my name was not on any of the documents, only my husband's.

I asked why only my husband's name was on the documents. I pointed out that I was the one paying the mortgage, as I was the one working. My husband was not working outside the home then but working on a book he was writing. I was told I need not be concerned as there was no issue with it being in my husband's name: I could make all the payments from our joint account, and it was customary to put homes and home loans in the husband's name, not the wife's. I was also told that it would take a week or more to redraw the papers and that the delay may cause us to lose the piece of land we wanted to buy.

Deep down inside, this little voice said, Hey, wait a minute. My name should be on there too. I am a person just as much as my husband. I am making the payments, and it is our house, not his house. But that voice was way down deep. It was so faint that I could hardly hear it. Then, it drifted off as I considered the potential loss of the land we had selected. And what was the problem anyway? We were married and happy, right? Who cared whose name it was in? I just went with the flow again.

I continued working and paying off the mortgage. I even went back to school. I didn't have a plan, but I always regretted not going to university when I was younger. Now that I was staying in one place, owned a home, and had a great job, I went to university and loved it. No plan, no problem. What could go wrong? I could worry about the future later. Well, when "later" came, it was devastating. I had no plan, no money, no home, and nowhere to go. What happened? My husband asked for a divorce.

The divorce happened in Georgia, and as the house was in my husband's name, it was considered his separate property, not marital property. It is possible that I could have fought this, but that would have been costly, and I didn't have the money for legal fees. To make matters worse, my car loan and my husband's were in my name. I ended up paying for both, even though I only got one of the cars. I was also emotionally devastated and not in the right frame of mind to fight over money when I had a broken heart.

I had a friend who had a rental property, and I moved, with my three children, into this home and started working to rebuild my life. But even after all of this, I still had no plan. I was severely depressed, drinking too much, not eating well, not saving, and not planning. I was getting by day to day, hoping for the best. I had hit rock bottom.

In 2002, my father became very ill and passed away. I managed to get to Australia to see him for a couple of weeks before his passing, but then I had to get home to America, back to my children and job. After Dad's passing, I called my mom daily and asked how she was doing. For a few weeks, she said she was doing fine and had lots of support. Then, one day, I made that same daily call. She broke down on the phone and told me she couldn't do it. Her world had fallen apart. She could not live without him. Why was she still alive? Why did the sun insist on coming up every morning? My heart was breaking. When I asked what I could do, her answer was simple: Come home. Come home now.

My mother had never asked me to change my life for her. She let me run all over the world and have adventure after adventure. There was only one thing I could do: go home to Australia. My son was living with his father, so I packed up my two daughters and left for Australia as soon as possible—WITH NO PLAN.

Once home, I started to do better physically, emotionally, and financially. I had the support of my family and lifelong friends. It was 2002, and my brother and I purchased a house together. I bought the house, and my brother renovated it. After a while, I purchased a second house and sold the first house, and my brother renovated the second house. It was a great partnership.

In 2004, my brother and I started a business together called Green Living Australia. I worked full-time for a big insurance company during the week and worked evenings and weekends in our little start-up business. Things were going well. In 2007, I purchased land, hoping to build a home in the country someday. The land I bought was the same size and very similar to the land I had and then lost in Georgia.

Overall, things were starting to go well. My children were growing up and becoming independent. My company was doing well, so I quit my job and worked in my business full-time. I was doing all right on both physical and financial independence. My weak point was emotional independence. I was lonely in my own company and the company of others. I made a conscious decision to find someone to share my life with. Having been burned once in a relationship, in 2011, I moved the property I had purchased in the country into a family trust. I was terrified of losing my home again. I started dating a man in 2012 and became engaged to him in 2015.

The entire time I was in this new relationship, I maintained separate finances and separate houses. In 2019, we ended our relationship. It had been a considerable drain on me emotionally and financially. I now believe that I made a mistake in selecting my life partner because I was emotionally dependent, did not love myself, and had probably chosen a partner who could not love me. I was once again emotionally devastated, but at the same time, it was a relief to have ended a relationship that was not going anywhere.

In 2021, I was served with divorce papers from the man I had been in a relationship with but had never been married to. We had been in a relationship from mid-2012 to mid-2019, a total of seven years.

We had been engaged for four years. He claimed we had been in a de facto relationship for eleven years. This predated my starting to go out with him, but hey, everything is a negotiation, so ask for more than you could be entitled to and see what you get, right?

So, what is a de facto relationship? Based on a quick search on the internet, in Australia, a de facto relationship is when you and your partner have a relationship and live together as a couple but are not married.[1] The five factors to be considered in establishing whether a de facto relationship exists are:

- Financial aspects of the relationship
- Nature of the household
- Social aspects of the relationship
- Presence or absence of a sexual relationship
- Nature of the commitment

Based on the above, point one is out as we maintained separate finances. My relationship was with a man on a disability pension, which he continued to draw. That was his decision. He did not want to be married or be in a de facto relationship so our relationship would not affect his pension.

Regarding point two, we both maintained our own homes, though there was plenty of visiting back and forth.

Regarding points three and four, friends and family considered us a couple in late 2012, and we became engaged in 2015.

On point five, this commitment was never made despite my wanting a real marriage. I firmly believe that a de facto relationship is not a marriage and should not be considered the same. My somewhat controversial opinion is that you are either married or unmarried, and a de facto relationship is not an equal substitute for marriage.

However, despite our separate households and finances, the relationship was enough for this man to claim a significant portion of my assets, even though he contributed nothing to the asset pool, never claimed to be in a de facto relationship, and continued to get paid by Centrelink as a single person. It is a hard reality to face that the law in Australia allowed this person to obtain a large settlement from someone he was not married to. He became a parasite even though he was not married and had not made a commitment. A sexual relationship lasting longer than two years, without children, living in separate households, and without joint finances can cost you significantly.

I managed to save my home and the home of my brother. (Yes, this man went after both.) Both homes were in my name due to my brother's disability, which didn't allow him to get a home loan.

This man also took all my superannuation, leaving me at sixty-one with only $5,000 for retirement. Injustices like this must happen every day. It doesn't matter if you are male or female; this could happen to you. And why did it happen to me? Because I had no plan. I was not planning for my long-term future. I was going with the flow, hoping for the best.

Could I have gone to court and fought this? Possibly, but the legal fees would have been more significant than I had the money for. My lawyer advised me that even if I won, I would never get my legal fees back as the other party would never be able to pay them. While this man could and did borrow money from his family to finance his case against me, I could not force his family members to loan him more money to pay my legal fees in the case that I won and was awarded these fees. So, no matter what I did, I would be wiped out financially. I had gotten into a no-win situation, and my lawyer advised me to settle.

What annoys me the most with this particular failure is that when I asked if his being on a pension as a single person made a difference, I was told yes. Still, at the same time, the court was not going to send any settlement report to Centrelink. It was up to the person receiving the money to self-report to Centrelink. Well, if a person never self-reported a de facto relationship to Centrelink, why would he self-report that he is claiming to have been in a relationship all of that time and now face a significant settlement? Would he volunteer to pay back the taxpayer? Does this system encourage fraud? Could I have prevented this from happening to me? With a plan, yes.

So, after having it all and losing it not once but twice, I finally understood what the universe was trying to tell me all along. You need to build the life you want. You need to have a plan. You need to run your life, or it will run you. You need to run your life like a business. If you want to build a business, you should start with a business plan, goals, and a vision for that business. So, to build the life you want, you need to have a life plan, goals, and a vision of what you want that life to be.

I finally got the message and decided to run my life like a business. The results have been spectacular. I went from having $5,000 for retirement to being financially independent and able to retire today if I wanted to, and I did it in four years. I have a successful investment portfolio, including cash, shares, and real estate. Even better, I also have minimal expenses. The combination of income and expenditures I have curated allows me to give generously to charity and travel overseas once a year. The rest of this book is my road map of how I did it and how you can too.

RUN YOUR LIFE LIKE A BUSINESS

The four primary areas of life can be broadly categorised. They are:

- Health, which includes physical, mental, and emotional well-being. It encompasses nutrition, exercise, sleep, stress management, and overall health maintenance.

- Wealth, which encompasses financial prosperity and security, including income, savings, investments, and managing debts.

- Relationships, which include our connections with other people, including family, friends, romantic partners, colleagues, and acquaintances. It involves aspects such as communication, trust, respect, and intimacy.

- Personal growth, which includes learning, self-improvement, and expanding our understanding of ourselves and the world. It incorporates areas such as career development, hobbies, and spirituality.

I have taken these four main areas and included steps you can take in each to create the life you want. I have started small, giving you tasks that will move you gently in the right direction. If you focus on one step each week, you can get through the book in a year. Some steps may take longer, depending on your current situation. Moving to the next step is OK while still working on an earlier one. For example, I talk about getting out of debt in week twenty-five. I don't expect you to pay off all your debts before you can go to step twenty-six, but you should have a plan of how you will get out of debt and have started working on it.

If you commit to following these steps, week after week, and maintain the previous steps while moving on to the next, your life will be changed entirely. The trick is to keep the gains you make as you go along. For example, I talk about exercise in week eight. If you only exercise for a few weeks and let it drop by week eleven, this program will not work. We are talking about changing your life. Successful people have a plan; they have habits that build one upon another, like a pyramid. If you let the earlier steps drop, your pyramid will collapse.

By the end of 2022, my "divorce" was finalised, and I had transferred my life savings to someone else. I then completed these fifty-two steps over a year, one step at a time. Some steps were easy; some were hard and even painful. I had to develop the steps as I went, not having them laid out for me. They were in numerous books, podcasts, and articles I read and listened to, but they were never put together in a usable package.

After completing these fifty-two steps, I live a fantastic life in my home, which is fully paid off. I replaced my life savings and have an investment portfolio. My business is thriving, and I spend time working and helping others. I have everything I wanted, and for the first time in my life, I truly love my own company. I want this for you. I want you to come with me on this adventure. Let's begin.

WEEK ONE: THE DAILY SCHEDULE

Change. But start slowly, because direction is more important than speed.

–Paulo Coelho.

My first step towards building the life I wanted was to set a daily schedule. You may need a different schedule from mine due to work commitments, family obligations, or other reasons, so tailor this to suit your situation. I have used my schedule as an example to help you set up yours.

Sleep is essential to an extraordinary life because sleep is essential for your overall health and well-being. Have a set time to get up in the morning and go to bed at night. Extraordinary lives don't start with sleeping all hours of the day, and they don't begin with late nights and not getting enough sleep. During sleep, your body repairs and rejuvenates itself, so getting enough sleep is essential for maintaining good physical and mental health, offering these benefits:

- Sleep is critical in maintaining a healthy immune system that fights infections and diseases. Lack of sleep has been linked to various factors, including obesity, diabetes, cardiovascular disease, and even early death.
- Sleep is essential for your mental health as well. It helps to regulate your mood, improve your memory, and enhance your cognitive function. Chronic sleep deprivation has been linked to depression, anxiety, and other mental health issues.
- Getting enough sleep can also help you perform better at work or school. It can improve your concentration, creativity, and productivity, allowing you to finish projects more quickly.

Get Up in the Mornings at a Set Time

I get up in the mornings at 5:00 a.m. I set the alarm for 4:45 a.m. and hit snooze. A second alarm goes off at 5:00 a.m. I love that fifteen minutes of half-awake and half-asleep time first thing in the morning. Having that little extra time before jumping out of bed makes me feel relaxed and like there is no rush. I can then comfortably get up at 5:00 a.m. This was not always the case, and it was a bit of a struggle at first. You might already be an early riser, or you may have difficulty getting out of bed in the morning. If that is the case, different strategies work for different people.

- Set an alarm. Without fail, always set the alarm before you go to bed. I use my mobile phone, which is charging overnight on my bedside table. I put the phone on flight mode so my sleep is not interrupted by random midnight messages. When a mobile phone is in flight mode, all wireless communication functions are turned off, including cellular network connectivity, wi-fi, and Bluetooth. This means the phone will not receive calls, messages, or notifications. However, the alarm function on a mobile phone usually works independently of wireless communication and does not require network connectivity. Therefore, in most cases, the alarm will still work even if the phone is in flight mode. It's worth noting that some older or basic phones may not have an independent alarm function and may rely on network connectivity to provide alarms.

- If you have trouble getting out of bed in the morning and often turn off your alarm, set multiple alarms. If you know getting up at 5:00 a.m. will be an issue, set an alarm at 5:00 a.m., one at 5:10 a.m., another one at 5:20 a.m., and another at 5:30 a.m. Do this the night before when you have the willpower to decide to get up at a particular time. Make it impossible to roll over and forget your good intentions.

- Set an alarm ten to fifteen minutes before you want to get up and then another alarm when you actually want to get up. This is what I do. I want to get up at 5:00 a.m., so I set one alarm at 5:00 a.m. and another at 4:45 a.m.

- Put your alarm in a different space where you can't reach it to turn it off. Before I got into the flow of getting up at 5:00 a.m., I put my phone in the connecting bathroom rather than on my bedside table. This stopped me from turning it off and going back to sleep. I had to get out of bed and walk into the bathroom to turn it off. By then, I was up and already in the bathroom, so I just got straight into the shower and started my day.

Go to Bed Each Night at a Set Time

I go to bed at 8:30 p.m., giving me eight and a half hours in bed. I aim for eight hours of sleep a night. Adults should aim for seven to nine hours, with women usually needing slightly more sleep than men.

I set an alarm that tells me when it is time to turn off the lights and go to sleep. This is necessary for me as I like to read in the evenings, and I can easily get so caught up in a book that I could read till 2:00 a.m. I have done this often, depriving myself of sleep and having a crappy next day. This was a bad habit that I had to break. Having that alarm go off tells me to put down the book and turn out the light. It took a bit of practice to get myself to do this consistently and not cheat. Now, it is a habit, and I never think twice.

There will always be exceptions to the times I have set. If I go out in the evening, I am up later. This is often the case for me on a Saturday night. In that case, I move my morning alarm for Sunday to a time relative to my Saturday night bedtime, just for that next day, to ensure I still get the eight hours of sleep I need for my health.

Schedule Some Morning "Me Time"

I get up at 5:00 a.m. and take about thirty minutes to prepare for my day: shower, dress, do daily skin care, and clean my teeth.

Create a schedule allowing time for whatever your morning routine entails. I don't particularly appreciate feeling rushed and don't want to skip essential self-care habits due to a lack of time, so I like to get up early.

Schedule Meal Times

Schedule three good meals into your day: breakfast, lunch, and dinner. Don't skip meals because you don't have time to eat.

I have set times to eat my three main meals daily, and I don't snack in between. I used to snack often, partly due to inconsistent mealtimes and skipping meals when I was busy. I have breakfast daily at 7:30 a.m., lunch at 12:30 p.m., and dinner at 6:00 p.m. If I stick to these times and never miss a meal, I don't get hungry in between.

To make this work, you must ensure that each meal is sufficient for your needs, which is different for men and women and can also change based on age, fitness, and activity level. Each meal must be balanced with enough, but not too much, of the three macronutrients: protein, carbohydrates, and fats. You do need all three of them; the trick is to have a balanced diet that fulfils your nutritional needs while at the same time being delicious. We will discuss what to eat in more detail in another step. For now, I want you to schedule a time in your daily routine to have three meals a day.

Another critical aspect of mealtime is to stop what you are doing and go somewhere to have your meal. Refrain from eating at your desk, in your car, or on the run. Take a meal break to sit down and enjoy your food. You must allow enough time to prepare and eat your meal peacefully. Eating on the run or quickly without taking the time to chew and savour your food properly can harm your health.

Here are my top four reasons to slow down mealtime:

- When you eat quickly, you tend to eat more than your body needs because your brain doesn't have enough time to register that you're full. It takes approximately twenty minutes after you start eating for your brain to get the message that you are full. Not eating your food slowly can lead to overeating and weight gain.

- When you eat quickly, you may not chew your food properly, making it more difficult for your digestive system to break down the food and extract nutrients. This can lead to digestive problems, such as bloating, gas, and constipation.

- Eating on the run may make you more likely to choose unhealthy fast-food options, often high in kilojoules/calories, saturated fat, and sodium. These foods can increase your risk of heart disease, diabetes, and other health problems.

- Eating on the run can also be stressful, increasing your cortisol hormone levels. High cortisol levels can lead to weight gain and other health problems, such as high blood pressure and a weakened immune system.

I allow thirty minutes to eat my meals. For example, my breakfast time is 7:30 a.m. to 8:00 a.m. That works for me because I work from home. If you leave home to work, your breakfast time may be earlier to allow you travel time.

Schedule Your Work Time

Your work schedule should have a definite start time and, just as important, a definite stop time. All work and no play makes Jack a dull boy. While work is necessary from a financial point of view, and having meaningful work is directly related to your emotional and mental well-being, work should not be your only focus. Having a definite start and stop time will allow you to include leisure activities and downtime in your schedule.

Using my schedule as an example, at 8:00 a.m., I get ready for work. My work schedule is from 8:30 a.m. to 4:30 p.m., so I have thirty minutes to prepare for my workday. This could be looking over the day's plan, grabbing a cup of tea, or booting up my computer. I want to be ready to work at 8:30 a.m., usually when I get my first phone call from my office staff or business partner.

Most people work outside the home and have a set schedule. You need to turn up at a particular time and knock off at a particular time. If this is you, then this is your work schedule. You will need to incorporate travel to and from work into your schedule. Creating a schedule that includes getting up, eating, travelling, and arriving at work at a set time will ensure that you are always at work on time, avoiding problems with your employer for being late. I have had several employees who could not turn up on time. This caused stress for the employee, the employer, and the other staff, who had to cope with another person's job not being done. Being late is bad for you, your employer, and your team.

If you work for yourself, then your schedule will be less predictable. You may have to attend clients' offices or residences to carry out your work. In this case, travel time will vary depending on each different client job you take. Still, it is important to be where you say you will be when you say you will be there. Arriving at a client's office or home late is unacceptable; it will give you a bad reputation and harm your business.

When working from home, schedules are just as necessary whether you work for someone else or yourself. This might be as easy as a work schedule of 8:30 a.m. to 4:30 p.m., which I do, but it could also be broken down somewhat if appropriate.

While working from home was considered exclusive to the self-employed, remote working was already beginning to grow in the corporate world. The arrival of the COVID pandemic kicked the changing trend into high gear as everyone left the office and stayed home in an attempt to stop the spread of the virus. While this situation is still in flux today, all over the world, people are heading back to the office; however, it is unclear if things will go back to the way they were before the pandemic. Workers have had a taste of working from home and the work-life balance they believe this style of working brings to them. Much of this will depend on individual preferences, company policies, and government regulations. Only some people may head back to the office full-time. Some companies may adopt a hybrid model, where employees work from home part of the time and come into the office for specific meetings or events. Other companies may continue with remote work as a permanent option, especially if it proves to be more cost-effective and efficient for their operations.

Your schedule may be a mix of at-home work and working from the office, which must be reflected in your daily schedule. For example, I work from home on Mondays, Tuesdays, Wednesdays, and Thursdays and away from home on Fridays. When working from home, I like to cut my day into segments. I work from home doing administrative tasks (bookkeeping, ordering, etc.) for Green Living Australia, the company my brother and I started in 2004. I also write, blog, and teach. I do the administration for Green Living Australia in the morning and write and blog in the afternoons. I am always there to take calls, and when you do customer service, you can't control when you get those calls, but I try to split my day between the two main areas I work: administration in the morning and creative work in the afternoon.

Ensure a Set Finish Time for Your Workday

Another important thing about work is that there should be a finish time every day. For most people, there is a knock-off time if you work away from home. However, if you work from home, it can be very tempting to keep working. My advice is not to do it. When that buzzer goes off at 4:30 p.m., I am done working. By then, I have been sitting in front of the computer for eight hours, less the thirty minutes I leave my desk for lunch. That is enough for me. I get up, leave the desk, go outside, look around, and be in a different space. Give yourself a break.

I am not saying that you can only work eight hours a day. If you want to work more, you can, but it needs to be on a realistic schedule. I do not believe in missing meals and sleep to work more hours. I am OK with missing watching four hours of TV a night to work more hours. You might have a second job, a study schedule to keep, or a side hustle. All these things are OK. They must be added to your schedule, and you must keep in those meal breaks and enough sleep for good health.

Because I knock off at 4:30 p.m., I have one and a half hours before dinner. I want to eat at 6:00 p.m., so I have more than enough time to make a meal.

You don't have to schedule every moment of your day. This can be unscheduled time. I might water the garden or call my daughter or a friend. I have a few friends who would be on the drive home from work and would love to chat. I might check social media for personal messages or look in on my investments using my iPad while sitting on the couch and drinking tea. This is some unwinding time after work and before I go to the kitchen for dinner.

For me, dinner is at 6:00 p.m., and it only takes thirty minutes to eat and maybe enjoy a glass of wine. After dinner, I quickly clean up so the kitchen is ready for the next day. I'm not particularly eager to wake up to a messy kitchen with dirty dishes from the night before. By 6:30 p.m. or 7:00 p.m., I am done for the day.

I like to get ready for bed at about 8:00 p.m., so I do what I love best with the remaining time: I read. I do not watch TV or the news. I might watch a show if there is something I want to see. I have access to Netflix, Amazon Prime, and Disney Plus, and occasionally, there is something I want to watch. However, most of the time, I like to sink between the pages of a good book.

Below is a sample schedule for a person who works Monday to Friday. I have based this on my schedule, so the times I have put in exclude travel because I work from home. I have added a travel line for those who need to use it. The weekend would have the same time minus the parts of getting ready for and going to work. Weekends are always flexible, as social events may blow the schedule to bits, but that's life. I am not trying to create a schedule that will limit my life. I am trying to develop a schedule to simplify and enhance my life.

This is the beginning of a basic schedule. As we move through the book, we will add habits and daily rituals to help you live an extraordinary life and reach your full potential.

Example Daily Schedule Monday to Friday (for those that work five days a week)

WEEK ONE: THE DAILY SCHEDULE

Activity	Example (based on my schedule)	Notes	Your Schedule Time	Notes
Get up	5:00 a.m.			
Get ready for the day	5:00 a.m. to 5:30 a.m.	Shower, dress, etc.		
Breakfast	7:30 a.m. to 8:00 a.m.			
Travel				
Getting prepared for work	8:00 a.m. to 8:30 a.m.	Get tea, boot up the computer, and review the daily plan.		
Work	8:30 a.m. to 12:30 p.m.			
Lunch	12:30 p.m. to 1:00 p.m.			
Work	1:00 p.m. to 4:30 p.m.	Stop work. You have done enough.		
Travel				
Dinner	6:00 p.m. to 6:30 p.m.			
Get ready for bed	8:00 p.m.	Get changed for bed, wash face, clean teeth, etc.		
Lights out	8:30 p.m.			

To-Dos for Week One:

1. Make yourself a daily schedule that suits your situation.
2. Create alarms on your phone to help you keep your schedule.

A daily schedule is meant to ensure that you get enough sleep, but not too much, and that you eat three times a day. Don't skip meals, and don't eat while working or driving; sit down and enjoy your meal.

These may be baby steps, but they add up to something amazing. Congratulations on completing step one on the journey to a simple, organised way of living. You are one step closer to creating the life you want.

End of Week One Review

You now have a daily schedule to ensure you get enough sleep, but not too much. You eat three times a day, don't skip meals or eat while working or driving, and sit down and enjoy your meal. This schedule also allows you to arrive to work on time and leave on time.

WEEK TWO: WEEKLY, MONTHLY, AND YEARLY SCHEDULES

Now that you have a basic daily schedule, let's look at weekly, monthly and even longer schedules. While a daily schedule is the best place to start, there are things you need to do once a week, once a month, or even once a year. To run your life like a business, you must keep track of these things. You can do this in a few different ways:

- Purchase a diary. They come in two forms: calendar year and financial year. You can pick one up at an office supply store or stationary outlet. I am a stationary snob, so I went all out and bought one that is a bit fancy.

- Use an online calendar like Google, Yahoo, or Zoho. Whomever you have your email with should also provide a calendar to go with it. This is great because you can get email notifications of upcoming things you need to do.

- Use a desk calendar. These come in various sizes, so choose one that suits your work area and desk space. Once the month has been completed, you tear off the month to show the next following underneath.

I have used all three of these, and they all work well. I have settled on using the diary and Google Calendar. I like the feel and look of my fancy diary, but I also like the electronic version, which I can access online on my desktop, iPad, and phone. I use the online calendar as a quick reference. I can set reminders to be emailed to me and select how far in advance I want that reminder to arrive. For my diary, I have the same information as my electronic, online version, but I can add more details. For example, if I have put someone's birthday on my calendar online, it will appear again in my diary, but with additional information, such as ideas of what they might want for a gift.

What should you put on your weekly schedule?

For this book, I will assume that you work Monday through Friday. If you have a different schedule like me and work on weekends, you will need to adjust your weekly schedule accordingly.

Start with those weekly items that need to be done or life will fall apart. These are basics everyone has that if skipped will cause problems. Some examples are laundry and grocery shopping. Pick a day of the week that will work for you and add this to your diary/calendar. If you work Monday to Friday, you have a few choices of when you will complete your basic living activities: weekday evenings, Saturdays, or Sundays. I like to do these activities on Sundays. I can get up Sunday morning and throw a load of washing on, then head out to the grocery store or a weekend market to pick up the weekly supplies with a list I have already made—more on creating and sticking to a shopping list later.

There could be other things that you do every week. It could be a visit to a family member that you do weekly or biweekly. Add this to your diary/calendar. You might be a member of a group, church, or club, and if so, add the meetings you attend to the diary/calendar.

Example Weekly Schedule

Monday	Tuesday	Wednesday	Thursday	Friday	Saturday	Sunday
Work	Work	Work	Work	Work	Visit family	Gardening, shopping, laundry, church at 9:30 a.m.

What should I put on my monthly calendar?

Flowing on from the weekly calendar, you can now add monthly activities, such as those with family, groups, and clubs. As you continue to add items, a picture should emerge of your activity, or lack of activity, as the case may be. Don't stress, and don't start creating new activities now. All you are doing is getting organised and putting what you already do into your diary/calendar. Some people begin to get worried as they realise they have too much going on, while others worry because they have little activity to report. Keep going until you have all the weekly and monthly activities recorded.

I am a member of a stitching group that meets every other Tuesday evening. I am also a member of Zonta, a fundraising group that aims to improve the lives of women and girls. We have a meeting/dinner on the second Monday of the month at the local Returned Servicemen's League (RSL). These are on my monthly calendar so I can plan ahead and not miss important meetings.

The second category I add is bills to pay, and I only add them to my electronic calendar, not my diary. Where you add these will be up to you. As these are not activities but bills that need to be paid or will be directly debited from my account, I colour code them in a different colour than the activities. This makes them easy to see, so I can always ensure my bills are paid on time. I never want to miss a payment and pay a late fee to a big company because I forgot the bill was due and didn't ensure I had the money in the correct bank account.

The types of things in this category would include:

- House internet
- Mobile phone
- Electricity/power
- Health insurance
- Mortgage
- Car loan
- Credit card bill

Add every monthly bill to your calendar, diary, or both. Don't rely on your memory. Have written records of when each account is due, regardless of whether you need to do a physical transfer or if it is a direct debit. If it is a direct debit from your bank account or credit card, this reminder will enable you to ensure the funds are available. Banks make a killing off dishonour fees. If a direct debit goes wrong, you get hit twice, once by the bank and then again by the company you were trying to pay. Never have this happen to you again. Put all your bills on the calendar and look at your calendar at least once a day. You can also set reminders to be emailed to you and have your emails come to your mobile phone. Technology is here to make running your life like a business easier. Use it.

What should I put on my yearly calendar?

WEEK TWO: WEEKLY, MONTHLY, AND YEARLY SCHEDULES

Now that you have your weekly and monthly calendar sorted out, look at those things that happen less frequently. The first thing that comes to mind is birthdays. Start with your own and then add immediate family and then close friends. I don't put my birthday on Facebook for the world to see, nor do most of my friends and family. It's personal information that really shouldn't be out there. Because of this, I can't rely on Facebook to let me know of a friend's birthday, so I add them to my electronic calendar.

After I have entered all the important birthdays, I then look again at bills, but this time yearly accounts such as:

- Home insurance
- Car insurance
- Car registration
- Yearly subscriptions

There is little you can do about some of these bills. They are what they are, but you should review them in some cases to ensure you are getting the best deal. In that case, you should add a task to your diary/calendar to do a review two weeks before the bill is due. For example, two weeks before my home insurance is due, I have a task on my calendar to review this bill and ensure I am still getting the best value for money. I do the same thing with my car insurance. A few phone calls can save you hundreds of dollars, and if you add it to your calendar, you can ensure you get it done. It's your job, so add it to the calendar.

What about those odd things that aren't weekly, monthly, or yearly?

You need to add a few other things that fall between the regular weekly, monthly, and yearly schedules. For example, you might get your hair cut every six weeks. Make your next appointment on the way out the door and add it to your calendar. I always do this, and because I book way in advance, I get the pick of the times that day. My hairdresser is never bothered if I have to call and change the date or time because of something else coming up.

To-Dos for Week Two:

1. Purchase a diary or desk calendar.
2. Make yourself a weekly schedule.
3. Add your monthly items.
4. Add your yearly items.
5. Add your remaining items that aren't weekly, monthly, or yearly.

End of Week Two Review

Now, sit back and look at your diary/calendar. Well done! You are a step closer to running your life like a business and succeeding. Daily, weekly, monthly, and yearly schedules simplify life. No company would make appointments and then not write them down. No business would have bills coming in that were not expected and prepared for. If you run a company like that, you will soon fail. It's the same with life.

To make this work, keep steps one and two going as you move to the next step.

WEEK THREE: MEDICAL AND DENTAL APPOINTMENTS

Other categories of items to add to the diary/calendar are medical and dental. Do you have a medical condition that needs follow-up? Should you be getting a yearly physical? This will differ depending on whether you are male or female and your age. An annual physical is a great idea and goes on my calendar. What about your six-month dental exam and cleaning? How about your annual eye examination? I habitually schedule the next appointment on my way out the door. For example, I attend my six-month exam and clean at the dentist and then, on the way out, I schedule another appointment for six months out. I know that six months is a while away and that I may have to change it, but if I don't set the appointment, time gets away, and I end up missing the care I need.

Once, I had moved, so I went to an optometrist in a new place. I forgot to set an appointment on the way out the door from that appointment, so there was nothing on my calendar—big mistake. As I had put nothing on the calendar, and as you know, time flies when you are having fun, it turned out that I had not been for an eye exam in over two years. I am sure you have done this yourself and would like to be better organised so this does not happen again.

These appointments are essential. Your health is important. You need regular medical, dental, and sometimes optical care. If you already have these appointments made, add them to your calendar. If you don't, make those appointments that are appropriate to you. Get your health under control.

To-Dos for Week Three:

1. Enter your medical/dental/optical appointments into your yearly calendar/diary.
2. Schedule your six-month dental clean and check-up.
3. Schedule your yearly medical check-up (as necessary).
4. Schedule your yearly optometrist appointment (as necessary).

End of Week Three Review

Well done. It is much harder to have a great life if you have health problems. Your health should be a top priority for you. There should be no such thing as insufficient time or money to care for yourself. This is your life we are talking about.

WEEK FOUR:
HAVE A HOME OFFICE

You need a home office to run your life like a business. This is a room with a desk, or a corner of a room with a desk, a table, or whatever you can afford or have the space for. It is a place, however humble, that is your office. It is a place you go to do all those administrative tasks that modern life demands.

Everyone needs a home office, even if it is just a small desk or table in the corner of the living room or your bedroom. You need a place to have your computer, laptop, or tablet, whichever you use, to do all those administrative tasks like paying the bills. If you are lucky, you can have an actual office in your house. I live in a three-bedroom home; one of these bedrooms is now my office. Such luxury. This is my first time having a home office where I can shut the door.

Set up your home office now. You will need a desk, table, or another flat surface to work on. I have seen a home office on the far end of a dining room table. Your office will have a chair and your desktop computer or laptop. This is where that desktop calendar or diary will be. Ensure you stock your home office with the basics: pens, a pen holder, a stapler, and a document tray. It must look and feel like an office. That way, when you sit down at your desk or table, you feel like you are at work, the work of running your life like a business.

This is where you will sit to pay your bills, make phone calls to set up appointments, add items to your diary and calendar, update your schedule, and more. Sit in your office at least once daily to check your calendar and diary and see what you need to do that day and week. Check your email daily. You may get other important emails or bills via email if you have selected the paperless option. Check the physical mailbox daily to see what has arrived. Use the document tray to put the mail in so nothing gets lost. Then, when you sit at your desk, go through the mail that came in and take care of business.

To-Dos for Week Four:

1. Set up an office space in your home (desk or table and chair).
2. Set up your desktop computer or laptop.
3. Stock your office with the basics: pens, a pen holder, a stapler, and a document tray.
4. Sit at this desk or table once a day and check your calendar or diary and your email.

End of Week Four Review

Congratulations on setting up your new office. You can't be expected to get organised and run your life like a business if you don't have a home office or a workspace to handle the everyday administrative tasks required to live in the twenty-first century. We will get more into the administrative side of living later, and there will be more to do in the office. But for now, establishing an essential home office is a big step in the right direction. You are building the necessary infrastructure to run your life like a business.

WEEK FIVE: JOURNALING

Journaling changed my life. I know that might sound a little dramatic, but I cannot overemphasise how vital journaling was and is to my mental health and the management of my life. It is no accident that mental health professionals use journaling as a therapeutic tool. There are many books on the subject, and peer-reviewed articles on journaling and its benefits have been published in psychological journals such as *The Journal of Psychology*.

It is common practice to have people keep a journal when dealing with issues in their lives and trying to make a change. Journaling aims to track their progress and document how they feel about the process they are going through; it also helps them get their emotions on paper to understand them better. For example, weight loss programs often have people journal their progress. They include their weigh-ins, what they eat, how they stick to the diet plan and exercise regime, what went right that day, and what went wrong. These reflections help people focus on what is helping them achieve their goals and what is getting in their way. It may help you locate and isolate emotional triggers for eating, spending, or drinking, whatever it is that you are using your journaling to help get under control.

Journaling is such a great tool, and it should be used daily by everyone who wants to take control of their lives and be the best they can be. Isn't that everyone?

Journaling has many benefits. It:

- Helps you clarify your thoughts
- Promotes mindfulness
- Reduces stress
- Promotes personal growth
- Enhances creativity

It provides a safe space to explore your thoughts and feelings. When I write in my journal, it is like having a conversation with someone who will never judge me or violate my privacy. It allows me to think deeply about and thoroughly analyse a situation and helps me avoid knee-jerk reactions to the outside world that I might later regret.

I use journaling to help me solve problems. I write down the problem and then start writing solutions. Some of these solutions are realistic; some are not. I don't overthink it; I just start writing. Then, like magic, possible solutions start tumbling onto the paper, some of which are gold.

Jim Rohn, author of *How to Use a Journal,* says there is something magical about writing our problems down.[2] When you do, your mind starts working on solutions. Write them down. Documenting what is going on inside your head helps you figure things out. It creates a space between you and your problem, allowing you to look at it more objectively.

Journaling also helps you capture good ideas. We all have many great ideas throughout our lives, but most are never acted upon and often forgotten by the next day or two. Use your journal to write them down. Don't rely on your memory. You might not be able to act on a great idea you have right away but you sure don't want to lose that idea when you could be in a position to turn that idea into a reality in the future.

I mentioned earlier that I am a stationery snob. When it comes to a journal, you should be a stationery snob too. Get something nice. It doesn't have to be expensive, but make sure you like it. I wouldn't go for the cheap exercise pad for this one. This is different to and separate from the diary. I use one that has no dates and no headings. I don't want a set amount of space per day. Some days, I might only write half a page. I might need a few pages on other days to clarify my thoughts.

It might take a little while to get into the swing of things and decide what to include in your daily reflections.

Here are some ideas to get you started. After noting the day of the week and date, answer these seven questions:

- What did you do today?
- How did your day turn out?
- What went well?
- What could have gone better?
- How do you feel?
- Did you make any progress towards your goals?
- What do you plan to achieve tomorrow?

I journal using these seven questions on the right-hand page. I save the left-hand page to write down ideas I come up with or find from others or through reading. I also write down inspirational quotes. I write my goals in the front of my journal and keep track of how I am doing towards those goals.

Journaling is a personal journey, so you can add to this in any way you like. I know people who write poetry in their journals, dinner ideas, and even sketches of things they want to create. I am guilty of adding to-do lists for the week ahead, ideas for writing blog posts, and books I want to buy and read.

The next step is to review your journals from time to time. See how far you have come. Catch up on these great ideas you've recorded. Are you ready to implement any of them?

This week, go out and get yourself a nice journal, one that will be a pleasure to write in. If you don't have a nice pen, get one. You can spend a lot on journals or get something under $5 from a discount store.

Once you have your journal, set a time on your daily schedule to do your daily reflections.

Update your schedule as indicated in bold below.

WEEK FIVE: JOURNALING

Activity	Example (my schedule)	Notes	Your Schedule Time	Notes
Get up	5:00 a.m.			
Get ready for the day	5:00 a.m. to 5:30 a.m.	Shower, dress, etc.		
Breakfast	7:30 a.m. to 8:00 a.m.			
Getting prepared for work	8:00 a.m. to 8:30 a.m.	Get tea, boot up the computer, review the daily plan.		
Travel				
Work	8:30 a.m. to 12:30 p.m.			
Lunch	12:30 p.m. to 1:00 p.m.			
Work	1:00 p.m. to 4:30 p.m.	Stop work. You have done enough.		
Travel				
Dinner	6:00 p.m. to 6:30 p.m.			
Journaling	7:45 p.m. to 8:00 p.m.	Daily reflections		
Get ready for bed	8:00 p.m.	Get changed for bed, wash face, clean teeth, etc.		
Lights out	8:30 p.m.			

To-Dos for Week Five:

1. Purchase a journal that you like.
2. If you don't have a nice pen, get one.
3. Select a time to do your daily reflection and add it to your daily schedule.
4. Using the seven questions above as a guide, start journaling daily.
5. Review your journal from time to time.

End of Week Five Review

Each week is like a building block. As you progress, don't let the good work of the previous weeks get lost. Review your progress and keep all your previous work going. If you let it drop, you must return and do it again.

WEEK SIX:
MAKE A NIGHTTIME RITUAL

When I wake up, I want to be enthusiastic and adventurous for the day ahead. To do that, I need to have a few things in place from the day before to make that great day happen. Creating small habits in the evenings can significantly impact the following day. Not having some of these things in place can sabotage your day before you start. Let's look at two ways to start your day, both good and bad.

Not the best way to start your day:

You wake up in the morning, hit the shower, and then arrive back in your bedroom wrapped in a towel, ready to get dressed. You open the wardrobe to select what to wear and have to decide. The shirt you are looking for to go with those pants you selected is nowhere to be found, so you pick something else, but the dress you pulled out needs to be ironed. On your third attempt, you see something that will work. You get dressed and head to the kitchen.

You arrive in the kitchen only to find a mess from the night before. You have to clear a space on the counter to make breakfast, and you wish you had loaded the dishwasher before bed. You eat while standing up, loading the dishwasher at the same time. Finally, you are ready to head out the door, so you grab your mobile phone only to realise that you didn't put it on charge last night, so it is flat. How do you feel about your day so far?

Right way to start the day:

By implementing some nighttime rituals, you can avoid the above drama in the morning and ensure a great start to the day. You must design your evening to get the morning you want, setting you up for success. To do this, you must create some evening habits that make the morning an easy, no-decision zone.

You have already created a schedule that includes three meals a day, and one of these meals is breakfast. You should have the ingredients on hand from your weekly shopping. Make breakfast easy by always having a clean kitchen before bed. Tidy up after dinner, load and start the dishwasher, and wipe down the counters. When I walk into my living area and see a clean kitchen, I have a much better start to my day than when I walk into a messy space. Your environment impacts your mental well-being, so start your day in the best state of mind and have a space that helps you do that.

Picking out what you will wear and laying out your clothes the evening before removes the need to make that decision in the morning. It also means you have the time to ensure you have what you need, not just for making the decision but also for pulling the clothes out and setting them aside. That way, you don't find out in the morning, when you are usually on a tight schedule, that the shirt you wanted to wear has a missing button. What you wear is important to how you feel about yourself. Make it a habit to select what you will wear the next day, the evening before, considering what you will be doing that day and the weather report.

Journaling at night helps you reflect on the day just passed and plan for the next day. Every night, I know exactly what I need to do the next day. Before I go to sleep, I have a plan and wake up in the morning ready to execute that plan. This plan isn't just in my head; it's a written one I can check off during the day. I don't wake up thinking about what I have to do that day. The evening before, what you need to do is fresh in your mind. It might include calling someone back, finishing a project you didn't get to finish the day before, or picking up a gift for someone's birthday. Important things from the day before are constantly forgotten without a prompt to remind you. People don't plan to forget; they forget to plan.

A better morning would be getting out of bed, hitting the shower, returning to your bedroom, and getting dressed in the clothes you picked out the night before. No decision, no stress. Then, you walk out into a clean kitchen for breakfast. You already know your plan of attack and are ready to take on the day on your terms. Not everything will go according to your plan. Life happens, but you are far less likely to forget important things if you wrote them down the evening before.

You may have other things in your nighttime ritual. You would want to brush and floss your teeth. You may have an evening skincare practice you wish to include. Whatever it is, make it a habit that you don't skip.

To-Dos for Week Six:

1. Create a nighttime ritual that becomes a habit.
2. Write this ritual down.

3. Be sure to include having a clean kitchen for the morning, picking out the next day's clothes, charging your phone, and planning for the next day.
4. Add in any additional items that are meaningful to you.

End of Week Six Review

Well done on another step to running your life like a business. Some of these steps seem small, but minor changes to your life have significant impacts when added together and compounded over time. Extraordinary lives don't happen by accident; they are planned and worked for.

WEEK SEVEN: CREATE A HABIT TRACKER

In the previous six weeks and steps, we have been creating habits, some of which you may have already had in place. In his book *Tiny Habits*, BJ Fogg talks about how critical tiny habits are and how they add up to significant changes.[3] The habits we have been introducing are each in themselves not earth-shattering. But together, as we add one to another, we get a different life from the one we were leading. You are now on a schedule, have three meals daily, and have an office to run your life like a business. You can review the past steps at the end of each section to ensure you're still following them. The best way to do this is to create a habit tracker that you can use daily or weekly, as the case may be. I do this for new habits I am trying to establish, so my tracker will change over time. After a while, when a habit is fully established, I no longer need to track it. New habits need additional attention, which a habit tracker is really helpful with.

Here is a quick habit tracker you could set up for yourself.

Habit	Mon	Tue	Wed	Thurs	Fri	Sat	Sun
Pick out the next day's clothes.	✓	✓		✓	✓	✓	✓
Load and run the dishwasher after dinner.	✓		✓	✓	✓		
Complete a journal entry and to-do list for the next day.	✓	✓	✓	✓	✓		✓
Floss teeth.	✓	✓		✓	✓	✓	

What you put on your habit tracker will be specific to you. For example, I never need to track "go to bed on time" as this is never an issue, though it used to be. But it took me a while tracking the habit of loading the dishwasher and turning it on in the evening before it became automatic. Fogg also says that behaviours equal motivation plus ability plus a prompt.[4] While I was motivated to do the dishes, and I was able to do the dishes, I would forget. So, I had to set a prompt to do it. I used my habit tracker to help with this. I decided that after I finished eating, I would always take my plate to the kitchen, which was my prompt to load it into the dishwasher. Then, before I did anything else, I would finish loading the dishwasher and start it.

I added my habit tracker to my journaling habit in the evening, and this helped me get the new habit of doing the dishes before bed locked in. I would stand back, look at that clean kitchen, and smile at a job well done. It greatly impacted my mornings and how I felt about myself. As I added new habits, I would add them to my habit tracker. As habits became locked in, they would drop off my habit tracker as I no longer needed the reminder. This is how a small change, like a habit tracker, can change your daily life. And those daily changes turn into life changes.

To-Dos for Week Seven:

1. Create a habit tracker for yourself.
2. Add the habits you are trying to incorporate into your life and need help with.
3. Add the habit tracker to your end-of-day journaling practice.
4. Update your habit tracker as needed.

End of Week Seven Review

You are doing great. Take a bow. Your new life is taking shape. Make sure that you are following each of the previous steps. You can't build a great life on a shaky foundation. You now have a daily, weekly, monthly, and yearly schedule, including necessary medical and dental appointments. You have a home office. You are journaling daily and have a nighttime ritual and a habit tracker. Each small step builds upon the next and will begin changing your life without the stress that can be caused by trying to make big changes that become unsustainable.

WEEK EIGHT: EXERCISE

We are told repeatedly that exercise is good for us, yet many are just not listening, or if we are, we do not make it a priority in our lives. I knew I needed to exercise. I had a job where I sat at a desk for eight hours a day, which was very unhealthy. But still, I put off exercise as I didn't have the time or the energy to make it happen. I kept telling myself that once my life improved, I would have time to do thirty minutes of exercise daily. But years passed, and it never happened. I was still too busy for myself.

I want you to think about that. This is your life, and exercise is vital to staying alive. If you don't have thirty minutes a day to stay alive, what are you doing here? A quick internet search will give you multiple reasons why exercise should be one of the top priorities in your life. Here is a short list of some, but not all, of the reasons exercise is good for you:

- Exercise can strengthen the heart and improve blood circulation, improving your cardiovascular health and reducing the risk of heart disease.

- Regular exercise can help you maintain a healthy weight or lose weight, if necessary.
- Exercise can build muscle, improve flexibility and posture, and reduce the risk of injury.
- Exercise can lower the risk of chronic conditions like diabetes, high blood pressure, and some cancers.
- Exercise can reduce stress, anxiety, and depression symptoms and boost self-esteem and cognitive function, improving your mental health.
- Regular exercise can improve the quality of your sleep, helping you feel more rested and alert during the day.
- Exercise can increase energy levels, boost mood, and improve overall well-being, leading to a higher quality of life.

I like to exercise in the morning. It sets me up for a great day. By 5:30 a.m., I am showered, dressed, and heading out the door for a walk. There are lots of things you can do to exercise. You could do a morning walk as I do, do a yoga routine, go to a gym for a morning workout, or use a home gym if you have one.

I have a knee injury, so I have taken running off my list. The knee injury also makes yoga difficult, but I have recently discovered chair yoga. My favourite exercise is taking a morning walk. I live in the country, so the morning walk is beautiful. Living in the country also means that driving to a gym in the morning is too far for me to travel. You might live close to a gym, making it a great option.

Exercise is the next thing I want you to put on your daily schedule. The question is, when? There is no one-size-fits-all answer. It depends on your personal preferences, schedule, and lifestyle. However, there are some potential benefits to exercising in the morning:

- Exercise can boost energy levels, and starting the day with physical activity may help provide a burst of energy to carry you through the day.
- Morning workouts may be easier to stick to as they are less likely to be disrupted by other commitments that may arise throughout the day.
- Exercise can help regulate the body's natural sleep-wake cycle, and morning workouts may help promote better sleep at night.
- Exercise can help boost metabolism, and working out in the morning may help jumpstart your metabolism and keep it elevated throughout the day.
- Morning exercise mentally sets you up for the day, releasing feel-good neurotransmitters called endorphins.

It is important to note that the benefits of exercise are not limited to morning workouts. Finding a time that works best for you and your schedule is more important to ensure consistency in your exercise routine. While I have selected morning exercise for the above reasons, this is only possible for some. Pick a time that works for you and an activity you will enjoy. It is much easier to stick to an activity that you like.

Looking back at the daily schedule we made in week one, you can see that I am ready for the day by 5:30 a.m. I put my earplugs in, pop on a podcast I want to hear, and head out the door. I want to do a minimum of thirty minutes, so I set the alarm on my phone for fifteen minutes and walk as far as possible before it goes off. I can return after fifteen minutes, getting in a thirty-minute walk, or keep going. Some days, it is just too beautiful to head home.

As time passes, you might need to change your exercise routine. Add more or take some away. I found that when winter set in, I was not so eager to go for morning walks, so while I was still motivated, it was just too hard. It was cold and dark at 5:30 a.m. My solution was to make exercising in the winter easy. I bought a treadmill. It is perfect for cold, wet, windy days and winter mornings when it is still dark at 5:30 a.m. and I can't see where I am going.

I hope you are convinced of the need to exercise and know you are worth thirty minutes daily. You deserve this time for your physical and mental well-being. Feeling great is part of an extraordinary life. So, get up, go out, and get it.

Here is my updated schedule, including exercise, as noted in bold.

WEEK EIGHT: EXERCISE

Activity	Example (my schedule)	Notes	Your Schedule Time	Notes
Get up	5:00 a.m.			
Get ready for the day	5:00 a.m. to 5:30 a.m.	Shower, dress, etc.		
Exercise	**5:30 a.m. to 6:00 a.m.**	**Walking**		
Breakfast	7:30 a.m. to 8:00 a.m.			
Getting prepared for work	8:00 a.m. to 8:30 a.m.	Get tea, boot up the computer, review the daily plan.		
Travel				
Work	8:30 a.m. to 12:30 p.m.			
Lunch	12:30 p.m. to 1:00 p.m.			
Work	1:00 p.m. to 4:30 p.m.	Stop work. You have done enough.		
Travel				
Dinner	6:00 p.m. to 6:30 p.m.			
Journaling	7:45 p.m. to 8:00 p.m.	Daily reflections		
Get ready for bed	8:00 p.m.	Get changed for bed, wash face, clean teeth, etc.		
Lights out	8:30 p.m.			

To-Dos for Week Eight:

1. Select a physical activity you can do every day for thirty minutes, such as walking, yoga, etc.
2. Select a time you will do this activity every day.
3. Add this to your daily schedule.
4. Adjust as necessary.
5. Do this daily exercise consistently, using a habit tracker as necessary.

End of Week Eight Review

You are eight weeks in now, or you might be moving faster. If you are, that's great. Most of what you have been doing so far has been organisational: making schedules, setting up an office, and writing in a journal. Now, you are getting out there, walking, going to the gym, or hitting the pool. You should be starting to feel these steps building upon one another while at the same time not feeling like you have had to make overwhelming changes and feeling destabilised. Baby steps.

WEEK NINE:
FOOD AND MINDFUL MEAL PLANNING

The food you eat should enhance your life, not make you sick. Top priorities should be planning, purchasing, preparing, and eating healthy foods. Yet, much like exercise, this is another area many people neglect. The biggest reason I hear is that people don't have enough time. It makes no sense that people don't have the time to take care of one of life's most essential activities: feeding themselves good food. It's one of the big three, food, clothing and shelter, yet I was among those people who didn't have the time. When I was hungry, I would put whatever was convenient in my mouth and suffer the consequences. It took a lot of effort to educate myself and eliminate the bad habits I had formed. Changing how I ate had a considerable effect, and my love affair with food started when I began to care what I put in my mouth.

My first three books are all about food. Anyone who knows me knows that I love food. I love to shop for great fresh food at farmer's markets and grow fruit, vegetables, and herbs in my garden. I love to make good food, from cheesemaking to home preserving, bread-making, and fermenting. And I love to eat good food and drink good wine.

Food is one of life's great pleasures, so I advise you to refuse to accept that you do not have enough time for good food.

From a nutritional point of view, a healthy, well-balanced diet can reduce the risk of many diseases, often referred to as preventable or lifestyle diseases. These include:

- Being overweight and obesity
- Heart disease
- Stroke
- Type 2 diabetes
- Some types of cancer

No one gets up in the morning and says, "I will eat food today that will give me a stroke." Yet millions of people do just that every day. Why? Because they don't have a plan, a food plan. They are just going with the flow, eating on the run, and fixing what is quick and easy. Earlier in week one, we did a daily schedule so that you would eat three meals and not eat at your desk or on the run. Now, we will be drilling down into what those three meals a day should be for optimal health and a great life.

Sit down once a week and make a menu. I like to do this on a Friday night, so I can get what I need from the store on the weekend, and of course, the Sunday morning farmer's markets where the best fruit and veg can be had at the best prices and usually grown locally. In weekfive, we added journaling to the daily schedule. I make my meal plan for the following week as part of my Friday night journaling. It helps me to stay organised when I keep everything in one place. It also allows me to go back and look at previous weeks for food ideas.

Planning avoids emergencies. I only plan out three meals a day. I don't snack between meals, so I don't need to plan for snacks. If you do a snack between meals, you also need to prepare for that. Otherwise, you may find yourself reaching for junk food when out and about, or worse, having junk food in your home for emergencies.

You will plan out breakfast, lunch, and dinner at a minimum. I find breakfast easy to plan, as I usually have the same few things on rotation. I eat oatmeal, eggs on toast with mushrooms, yoghurt with fruit, or sourdough pancakes. Lunch is also easy as, once again, I eat the same few things on rotation. I eat a cheese and salad sandwich, cheese on toast with Kimchi, or a cheese and pickle sandwich. This suits me well as I love cheese and prefer a vegetarian diet for the most part.

Dinner takes a little more thought, but it doesn't have to be complicated. I see people attempting to make a meal plan for the first time, and they get out cookbooks, trying to find recipes to add to their list. This is the wrong way to go about meal planning. You want to include tried and true recipes that you know you love. Add family favourites and meals you already know how to make. Get a list of half a dozen or so to get you started.

I have included an example for you below. This is based on my weekly meal plan, but I have slipped in a few non-vegetarian meals to give you a better idea of the possibilities. My sample meal plan starts on a Saturday, as I usually plan on a Friday evening.

Example Meal Plan

Day	Breakfast	Lunch	Dinner	Notes
Saturday	Eggs on toast with mushrooms	Cheese sandwich with salad or pickles	Homemade pizza. I make the sourdough base.	I make my bread and pickles. I grow salad greens in my garden.
Sunday	Sourdough pancakes	Cheese sandwich with salad or pickles (change up the cheese and toppings)	Pasta (try tuna-noodle casserole)	If you don't have time to make it from scratch, pasta, tuna, and canned mushroom soup will do.
Monday	Oatmeal	Tuna salad sandwich (you can make tuna salad with just tuna and mayonnaise)	Curry (try my Green Pawpaw Coconut Curry on my blog)	Papaws are everywhere in Queensland. When not in season, try potato and cauliflower curry.
Tuesday	Baked beans on toast (with or without an egg)	Sandwich	Shepherd's pie (meat or vegetarian-based, topped with mashed potato)	I use only vegetables thickened with lentils, but you could add minced beef.
Wednesday	Homemade yoghurt and fresh fruit	Tuna melt sandwich	Roast chicken, potatoes, green beans, and carrots	Pick up the roast chicken on the way home from work. Vegetarian option: Zucchini fritters in place of the chicken.

Thursday	Yoghurt and muesli	Chicken salad sandwich (use leftover chicken)	Chicken and vegetable soup with potatoes, carrots, beans, and sweet corn	Take the remaining chicken (bones and all) to make chicken stock and add vegetables to make soup. Vegetarian option: Leave out the chicken and use vegetable stock cubes instead.
Friday	Homemade yoghurt and fresh fruit	Sandwich	Leftovers or stir-fry if you don't have leftovers	I make my yoghurt.
Saturday	Eggs on toast with mushrooms		Homemade pizza (with homemade mozzarella)	It only takes me thirty minutes to make mozzarella.

If you like these ideas, check out the recipes on my blog.

https://livingsimplywithvalerie.com.au/

Once you have made your first meal plan, you can use it repeatedly without changing it, or you can edit one, two, or more of your weekly selections to have an even greater variety. I do this based on what is in season. I also grow vegetables in my garden so I can go out and pick fresh, in-season food all year round. Eating seasonal fruits and vegetables is good for you, saves you money, and is good for the environment.

As you continue meal planning every week, you will add more to your choices. You can even get out that cookbook after a while and add something new to the list that might become your next family favourite. I enjoy cooking, and I like to try new things. I just don't want a meal plan full of new things. I need my meal plan to make my life easier, not more complex.

Once you have your meal plan, it is time to make your shopping list. The key is planning, making a list, buying only what you need, and using everything you buy. Make a list using your plan and check what you already have on hand. Some people can only shop once a week. Others can shop more often, doing smaller shops throughout the week. Either way, make a list, take the list, and stick to the list. Never go shopping while you are hungry.

I have been doing this for some time now and have developed a list of basics I always have on hand. I can use this list to ensure I always have what I need, including spices I regularly use, canned items I might want to stock up on when there is a sale, and dry goods I can get in bulk to save money.

Food Basics List

- Milk
- Eggs
- Mushrooms
- Bread: Making your own is even better.
- Cheese: You can make your own, but it is not cheaper than a plain cheddar style you can get for under $10 per kilogram.
- Butter: I never use margarine.

- Pickle or chutney: I make my own.
- Bread flour: Use this for bread-making and pizza dough.
- Plain flour: Use this for cakes and biscuits.
- Fresh vegetables: green beans (I grow my own and freeze them for winter), lettuce, and tomatoes (I grow my own). I make jars of pasta sauce in summer and autumn, enough to last me all winter and spring. In winter, I grow cauliflower and broccoli and make a cauliflower and broccoli cheese bake. I also blanch and freeze these winter veggies when they are free from the garden (or available inexpensively in the grocery store) to use later in the year when they are not in season and expensive.
- Root vegetables: potatoes and carrots. I purchase only what I need for that week. I always have onions and garlic on hand. They are the base for all my curries, soups, and stews.
- Fruit: I get free apples from my neighbour and make apple pie or baked apples in pastry. I stuff the core with honey and walnuts.
- Meat: Get a whole-cooked chicken if you are a meat eater. If you want to use minced meat in your shepherd's pie, get good quality, not the cheapest, which is full of fat.
- Canned goods: I always have some baked beans on hand.
- Jam: I make sugar-free jam. It's great on toast as a snack or mixed in with yoghurt, and it's also great on scones.
- Coconut cream and coconut milk: I use these in curries.
- Lentils: Great for thickening curries, soups, and stews.

- Spices: These four spices go into every curry: turmeric, coriander, cumin, and chilli.
- Salt and pepper
- Cooking oil: I cook with rice bran oil. I have olive oil on hand for pasta dishes and salad dressings.
- Tea and coffee: I drink loose-leaf tea, not tea bags, and have coffee for visitors.

Sometimes, I go to the store or market and see a great deal on something I can save or preserve for later use. This could be a good deal on tea or coffee that will last or something I can preserve, like strawberries I can turn into jam. This is one of those times when I don't stick to the list. These are always basics, as getting a good deal on something I end up not eating and throwing away is not a good deal.

Buy without packaging whenever possible. Some stores sell food without packaging. There are bulk stores where you can scoop what you need from a bin, without packaging. I do not buy packaged foods—no pre-prepared meals, cakes, or biscuits. If I want them, I make them. Kids love to bake. Get the family involved.

Why do I do all of this?

- For my health. Food made from scratch is usually better for you. If you use good, wholesome ingredients, there are no artificial colours, flavours, or chemical preservatives. It's your body, the only one you have. Look after it.
- I save loads of money. With a meal plan, I avoid purchasing pre-made, pre-packaged foods or junk food. Not only is highly processed food bad for you, but it can also be expensive.

- It's better for the environment. According to Oz Harvest, one-third of food produced in Australia is wasted, and the top five most wasted foods are vegetables, bread, fruit, bagged salad, and leftovers.[5] Remember, this is not your planet. You are just holding it in trust for your children and grandchildren. If you don't have any children, then you are holding it in trust for my children and grandchildren, and I thank you for it. Try to leave the planet in a better shape than when you arrived.

- It reduces my decision fatigue. Decision fatigue is the idea that the more decisions you have to make during a day, the more fatigued you will become. As that fatigue kicks in, your ability to make the right decision reduces. After a full day of working reading, writing, blogging, or speaking, I don't want to come home and figure out what I will have for dinner. I would instead look at my meal plan. Because I made a meal plan and then shopped based on that plan, I never have to worry that I don't have the ingredients. Having a meal plan makes my life easier. Besides, I have better things to consider, like where to take my next holiday.

To-Dos for Week Nine:

1. Decide when to make your weekly meal plan and add it to your calendar or diary.
2. Make your weekly meal plan.
3. Make a food basics list.
4. Make a weekly shopping list.
5. Go shopping and stick to the list. Don't buy junk food.
6. Keep the receipts.

End of Week Nine Review

Look back over the previous steps and make sure that you haven't let anything drop off. Are you still operating off your daily, weekly, monthly, and yearly schedule? Do you still sit at your desk at least once daily and check your calendar and email? Are you journaling and engaging in physical activity every day? Add step nine to the previous eight steps to become more organised and run your life like a business.

WEEK TEN: ONCE-A-WEEK MEAL PREPARATION

Now that you have a meal plan, you can get ahead by doing meal prep before the busy work week starts. I like to do my weekly meal prep on Sundays. I do my food shopping on Sunday, so each Sunday afternoon, I am in my kitchen with all my ingredients and a plan of what to make.

I can put a batch of yoghurt on. That only takes two minutes. I love vegetable curry, so I get one going in a big pot on the stove. I make more than I will use for one meal, so I can divide it into single-meal containers and pop them in the freezer for later. The kitchen is my happy place, so I can go crazy and make bread, whip up a batch of ricotta, or make homemade pasta. You don't have to get fancy if cooking is not your thing. You can keep it as simple as you like. It's all about cooking, dividing, and storing food to make it easier to eat healthy meals throughout the week. This is especially important for people with busy lives who may not have the time to cook a meal from scratch every night of the week. Meal preparation can include prepping ingredients, making complete meals, or a combination of both.

Weekend meal preparation has several benefits, including:

- Saving time
- Saving money
- Reducing food waste
- Assisting in maintaining a healthy diet

To get started, you will need some single-meal-sized containers to freeze meals in. I would not go for the disposable type but rather get good-quality ones that will last years. I would also get some labels to label every container's contents and the date it was made. Then, when you make a pot of curry, you can divide it into several containers. I use containers I can pull from the freezer and put straight into the microwave.

Let's look back at the list of example dinners from week nine:

Pasta (try tuna noodle casserole)	It can be pre-made and frozen.
Curry (try my Green Pawpaw Coconut Curry)	It can be pre-made and frozen.
Shepherd's pie (meat or vegetarian-based, topped with mashed potato)	It can be pre-made and frozen.
Roast chicken, potatoes, green beans, and carrots	Pick up chicken already cooked on the way home.
Chicken and vegetable soup with potatoes, carrots, beans, and sweet corn	It can be pre-made and frozen.
Leftovers or stir-fry if you don't have leftovers	It is better made fresh, but it is quick and easy.
Homemade pizza (with homemade mozzarella)	I make this fresh on Sunday night and freeze the leftovers.

WEEK TEN: ONCE-A-WEEK MEAL PREPARATION

Having a meal plan and getting all the shopping done is an excellent step in the right direction, but then doing meal prep sets you up for a great week where you can be super productive, not having to think about your meals because it is all sorted. Imagine getting home from work and not having to cook when you're tired and hungry. Imagine pulling a healthy meal out of the fridge or freezer. Organising reduces stress for busy people wanting to get things done.

To-Dos for Week Ten:

1. Purchase some good quality single-meal-sized containers to freeze meals.
2. Based on when you do your meal plan and shopping, pick a day to do your weekly meal prep and add this to your calendar.
3. Prep your meals for the week.

You won't perfect this in one week. If all you get done in the first week is to make one big pot of soup, curry, or spaghetti Bolognese and pack it into six meal-sized containers, that is a start. Next week, aim to get two items cooked. You will build up over time until you always have meals on hand for the week and never have to skip a meal, cook when tired and hungry, or order in because you are starving and there is nothing to eat.

End of Week Ten Review

Doing meal prep may have been your most significant change in the first ten weeks. How are you doing on weeks one through nine? Every step up to this point has helped you realise that meal prep is possible for you to consider. I know some people don't do meal prep, but they are wasting time and money by not doing it. You might not like this step when you first try it, but if you make this a habit, it becomes easy, and then you will start to see the benefits and wonder why you haven't been doing this all your life. For those who don't like cooking, meal prep means less time in the kitchen.

WEEK ELEVEN: MAKE A FOOD BUDGET

While my main reason for making meal plans and pre-preparing meals is to ensure a healthy diet and to save time, it is also a great way to reduce food waste and save money. After a couple of weeks of keeping the receipts from your food shopping, you should understand how much you need to spend each week on food to feed yourself and your family.

After working with hundreds of people who have attended my Mindful Meal Planning seminars, I can tell you that the size of your family is not the main determining factor in what you spend on food a week. It is how well you plan and prepare each week. For example, I have worked with families of four who have consistently spent over $400 a week on food, while another family of the same size will pay around $200. The difference was in the planning and the amount of pre-packaged processed foods purchased.

I recommend collecting at least five weeks of receipts to determine your average weekly food spend. Take the total you have spent per week and add it up. Then, divide the total by the number of weeks you have tracked. This is your average per week food spend.

In the example below, I have used five weeks, tracked the spending, and divided the total by five. This family's average food spend is $174.76. I would set the food budget for this family at $175 per week. This exercise aims to know what you spend per week on food. The result surprised some people, and most wished they could spend less.

Week	Amount Spent	Average
1	$178.62	
2	$164.98	
3	$204.79	
4	$153.27	
5	$172.15	
Total	$873.81	$174.76

In week eleven, we are just looking at our spending, not necessarily trying to reduce it. That will come later, if necessary. The first step in trying to get control of something is to know what you're dealing with. Set this money aside in a separate account for your grocery shopping or take it out in cash and put it into a food expense envelope. That is what you can spend per week. If you have money left over from the previous week, add it to the following week. This way, you will have a little extra cash when those great deals come along. Remember, it is not a great deal if you buy food you do not use, and it goes off; it wastes your hard-earned money.

To-Dos for Week Eleven:

1. Gather five weeks of grocery receipts or look at your bank statements and work out your weekly spending.

2. Based on the result of step one, set a weekly food budget.
3. Set up a separate account with a debit card for your groceries or withdraw the amount in cash each week and put it in a food expense envelope.
4. If you spend less, roll that money into the following week without reducing what you add to that account or envelope each week.
5. Stick to your new budget.

End of Week Eleven Review

This week was our first real week of getting into the subject of money. Money is an important consideration and a part of living a great life. Money does not buy happiness, but the lack of it can create significant misery. Working on a food budget before getting into the rest of your budget is an excellent start because food budgets are very flexible and an area where you can get an easy win with a bit of planning. It is also a bite-sized look at your finances, easing you into looking at the bigger picture later.

WEEK TWELVE: DECLUTTERING YOUR HOME

The environment we live in is important. It can affect how we see ourselves, as our homes are an extension of ourselves. Our personal space can have either a positive or negative impact on our mental health. Our homes should be a sanctuary where we can escape from the world when needed, a place to recharge our batteries and become even stronger. Our homes should be a safe space where we feel comfortable and content just to be there.

How do you feel about your home? Is it all that you want it to be? Unfortunately, for many people, this is not what our homes are. Homes have become a storage area for the stuff we accumulate. Equally unfortunate is the fact that we are accumulating at a faster rate than at any time in history. "Stuff" is more efficiently and economically produced in our modern, mass-production, global economy, and it is then aggressively marketed to us in the thousands of marketing messages we receive every day.

We all end up purchasing too much stuff—stuff we do not need, stuff we never use, stuff to make us feel better. Stuff does not make people feel better, but we have all practised what we call "retail therapy" at one time or another, only to find out later that the good feeling elicited by the purchase is short-lived. The credit card debt, however, lasts much longer.

Then, when you have all this stuff, what do you do with it? Why you store it, of course. We hang onto things we don't need for numerous reasons:

- We spent money on it, which gives it a perceived value.
- It was a gift, and we feel obligated to keep it.
- We might need it one day.
- We don't have time to sort everything out, so we keep it.
- We have a spare room, so we fill it. (Then we no longer have a spare room.)
- It has sentimental value.

Repeat after me: My home is not a storage unit. Say it again.

All this stuff is heavy, physically and mentally. When you start to get rid of it, you lighten your home and yourself. Stuff takes up time and energy to look after. You get to a point where there are things you want to do, but your stuff is stopping you. Don't spend your leisure time organising your stuff; get rid of it and spend your time having a life.

Start getting rid of your excess stuff. Tackle one area of your home at a time. I started with the bookshelves. I love books, but I had so many that there was no room to store any more. There were books on my shelf from thirty years ago that I had never picked up in all that time. There were some books that I had several copies of, but they were in different editions. I had three copies of *The Age of Innocence* by Edith Wharton. THREE! I didn't get rid of any book I truly wanted. They bring me great joy. But there is a limit to how many copies of the same book you need.

I then moved to the kitchen. I had about fifteen bread tins. Don't even get me started on the coffee cups. Week after week, I dropped a box off at the Salvation Army's second-hand store. Nothing went to the landfill. Everything went to charity. I kept what I truly wanted and used, and slowly but surely, my kitchen became a place that was a pleasure to work in, not an overwhelming mess of stuff stacked in cupboards and drawers where I could never find what I was looking for.

While I was motivated to do this, it was not easy. The stuff I got rid of came off in layers. Some weeks, I was not very good at letting go of stuff. In other weeks, I did better. It took me a month to get the bread tins down to the four I use. Each week, another bread tin would go in the box. Layer by layer, I reclaimed my home from years of clutter.

You can donate all this excess stuff to charity or organise a yard sale. I know people who have paid for a holiday with the money they got for all their excess stuff. That's not bad. But getting rid of the stuff is just the first step.

The second step is not to fall into the trap of replacing this stuff that you don't need with other new stuff that you don't need. Think twice before you spend your hard-earned money. Ask yourself, Do I need this? Don't fall victim to FOMO, the fear of missing out, which is used as a marketing tool designed to get your money out of your pocket. If you think you want that thing, wait till the following day and see if you still want it. Chances are the impulse to buy will have passed, and you will realise you don't actually want it. Companies rely on people's impulse buying, so don't do it. Save that money for something that will add value to your life.

What adds value to your life? It is seldom stuff. It is more often experiences like travelling, holidays, nights out with friends, courses taken, art galleries visited, the class on gardening you took, or going to a concert. These are the things memories are made of. At the end of my life, I will not think about whether I should have accumulated more stuff in my life or could have done with another pair of shoes.

We all have some things that are extra special to us. There are a few things I still purchase more than the average person. I buy at least a book a week. I read even more. I also have a library membership, so I can borrow books in addition to the ones I buy. I love books. I also love to garden, so I buy a new plant or tree every week. I have twelve acres, so I don't see this ending any time soon. But that is me. I love to read and garden. It is the experience of reading and gardening that I love. There are special books I read again and again. You get to keep what makes you happy. You get rid of what is holding you back, sucking up your energy for little or no return.

Need help reducing your stuff? There are websites dedicated to decluttering. There are books on decluttering. There are even courses you can take to help you declutter. You can hire someone to come to your home and help you make the tough decisions. You could start small and decide to get rid of one thing a day.

The one-thing-a-day method is a great way to start if you are struggling. Find a box and put it on the back seat of your car. This is the box that is going to go to Goodwill at the end of the week. Then, every day, pick one thing. Take it out of your house and put it in the box—just one thing. Don't think about how much decluttering you have to do. Just focus on taking one thing out of your house. Then, once you have taken that one thing, do a little dance. Congratulate yourself. You are terrific. How do you eat an elephant? One bite at a time.

To-Dos for Week Twelve:

1. Decide to start your decluttering journey.
2. Select the area you want to tackle first and begin decluttering it, removing stuff you do not need or use.
3. Alternatively, take one thing out of your house daily and put it in a box in your car.
4. Take the box to Goodwill at the end of the week or on the weekend.
5. Get assistance by looking online, reading a book, taking a course, or hiring help if needed.
6. Stop buying things you do not need.
7. Buy experiences instead of stuff. This is also a great gift idea.

End of Week Twelve Review

This week's subject may be challenging for some people. Clutter is a huge issue, evidenced by the large number of storage businesses everywhere. This week's topic may take you many weeks to complete. Just add the practice of decluttering to your weekly plan and do your decluttering consistently.

WEEK THIRTEEN: DESIGNING YOUR PERSONAL SPACE

Now that you have begun decluttering your home, it is time to design the space of your dreams. It doesn't matter if you live in the country, in suburbia, or in an apartment in the city; you can make your space suit your needs and personal taste. The first thing to do is get an idea of your taste. The stuff around you in the past was probably an assortment of things collected over time, gifts from others, and may or may not have been what you would have chosen for yourself. It was also probably way too much stuff. When it comes to stuff, less really is more. How do you find your ideal look and feel? There are a few different ways.

- Go through magazines to get ideas. Use the library.
- Use Pinterest.
- Check out home decorating and design books from the library.
- Go window shopping. Don't buy, just look.

Once you know what you want your home to look and feel like, you can start making it happen. One thing stands out when you look at stylised homes and photographs in books and magazines. No clutter. There is plenty of clean space. It is always quality over quantity. That does not mean that what you have needs to be expensive, but what you have needs to be well selected. Your goal here will be to own much less but have what you do own be things you need, use, and love. Everything you have should add to the quality of your life, not just need to be dusted. Life is about choices. Would you rather have a pile of stuff or a trip or a lifetime? More collectables or season tickets to…? You get to fill this in.

This process is going to take some time. Don't be in a hurry. Take it slow so you don't make the mistake of getting anything else that will end up being clutter. A blank canvas is better than a mess. Keep it simple. Keep it minimal. Remember, less is more. Enjoy the space and add to it slowly and carefully.

To-Dos for Week Thirteen:

1. Work out your style by looking through magazines, Pinterest, and books.
2. Take your time and add slowly to the blank canvas you are creating with your decluttering.
3. Only get things that add to your life, not things that add clutter.
4. Avoid impulse purchasing.

End of Week Thirteen Review

Congratulations. You are 25% of the way through the year and the book. Up to this point, we have been focusing on schedules, exercise, food, and the home environment. These are all designed to help you get your basics in. Not all of these steps have a specific end date. You may still be deciding on your home's style or continuing to declutter. You might be slowly building your meal prep practices. Just keep working on and continuing to do the first thirteen steps.

WEEK FOURTEEN: GOAL SETTING

Setting goals is an essential part of running your life like a business. Every well-run business has goals. These might be revenue goals, goals to release new products, or goals to acquire another business venture that would complement an existing business. Businesses that succeed do not just drift along, wondering where they are going and where they will end up. They have goals they wish to achieve, strategies to implement to get there, and plans to put in place. If you want a successful life, you need to do the same. The first step is to define your goals. What do you want? So many people don't know the answer to this question.

Your goals could be financial, such as the amount you want to have in savings. You could also aim to buy a car, own your home, or even take an extended overseas holiday. Your goal doesn't matter as long as it is genuinely what you want. Some people struggle to determine what they want from life. It is worth spending some time working out your goals.

The best way to work out your goals is to get a pad and pen and write down things you want to do, be, or have. Don't worry if they are realistic and achievable. Don't tell yourself that a goal is too big or too difficult. Be ridiculous if you want to. Have as many goals as you wish. Later, you can sort them out and filter them down to the few you want to work on. At this point, just start writing down goals. You may want to buy a new car, go back to university, get a better job, or save $100,000. The idea is to get your thoughts down on paper.

Once you have a good list of goals, you can start sorting them to see which ones are more important to you. What goals should come first? For example, you might have written a goal to get out of debt and another to go on a holiday. Which one should you do first? It's probably a better idea to get out of debt before you go on holiday. Sort through your goals until you have limited them to the three that would impact your life the most.

Some goals require a longer time to reach. Because of this, I set one-year and five-year goals. After losing my life savings for the second time, I made a five-year goal to become a millionaire. While I realise this is not as impressive a number as it used to be, I started with very little but a great amount of determination and, for the first time in my life, a plan. I accomplished this goal in four years because I ran my life like a business.

Here is a list of goals as an example.

- Buy a house
- Get out of debt
- Get a new car
- Go to Hawaii on holiday
- Lose ten kilograms

WEEK FOURTEEN: GOAL SETTING

- Write a book
- Read *War and Peace*
- Buy all new clothes (because you lost ten kilograms)
- Learn to play the cello

This is a short list; if you spent some time, you would have a longer list, but this will work as an example. Now, pick which goals you should start with.

I would choose the following three:

- Get out of debt. With lots of debt, it would be hard to get a home loan, so if I work on getting out of debt, I am also working towards buying a home. Getting out of debt would also help move me towards a new car and a holiday to Hawaii.
- Lose ten kilograms. I would pick this one before getting all new clothes, as getting new clothes and then losing weight would only mean I have a lot of new clothes that do not fit.
- My final goals are to read *War and Peace*, write a book, or learn to play the cello. I could go either way on this one. I have now read *War and Peace* and written a book, but I still don't play the cello. That makes me think it might not be as important as I once thought.

Some choices are more personal for the individual rather than based on logic. Whatever you choose from your list, make it meaningful to you.

So now you have three goals to work on. I usually keep my yearly goals to three. They can be big or small. The point is that I now have a destination in mind, something I am working towards, and a way to measure my progress towards the selected goals.

Check your progress on your goals once a week. This could be as simple as writing down your weight each week. Are you going in the right direction? Or writing down how much you still owe? Is this coming down every week?

Among everyone I have worked with, the most common goal was to get out of debt. This tells you something about the society we live in. So many people are drowning in debt, including student loans, credit card debt, car loans, etc. It is a world where we are constantly bombarded with advertising, creating "need" for unnecessary things; a world where we get the stuff before we have the money to buy the stuff and where we can roll credit card debt from one card to another and then dig ourselves into an even larger financial whole.

As I write this book, we are in a cycle of increasing interest rates. We face ever-increasing mortgage payments, rent rises, and cost of living increases, forcing some people into losing their homes. Debt is costly. There is good debt and bad debt. More on that later, but for the most part, it is best to avoid debt. If you can't afford something, you definitely can't afford that same thing plus crippling interest. Getting out of debt is a common goal, so we will discuss how to do this later.

You could make yourself a visual aid to motivate you. I use an Excel spreadsheet and the graphing function to visualise my progress or lack thereof. I made a one-year goal of having $50,000 in an investment portfolio. I looked at it at the end of every week and popped the number into the Excel spreadsheet, automatically creating the graph. This motivated me to take the necessary steps to put in more money as I began to see the growth from my contributions and the increased share prices of the selected investment. It became a game to reach my goal as fast as possible.

WEEK FOURTEEN: GOAL SETTING

This week is all about setting the goals that you will be working on in the next few years.

To-Dos for Week Fourteen:

1. Get a pad and paper and write down as many goals as you want. What do you want to be, do, and have? Don't filter this at this point; just write.

2. Once you have a good list, select three you want to work on for the year. What should come first? What would have the most significant impact on your life?

3. Work out how you can measure your progress towards these goals and track your progress in your journal once a week.

End of Week Fourteen Review

Your basics should now be well and truly in place, but if you have any doubt, go back and look at weeks one through thirteen. At the end of week fourteen, you have selected three goals you will be working on for the following year. Write them in the front of your journal and keep weekly track of your progress.

WEEK FIFTEEN: CREATING A VISION BOARD

Vision boards are a fun and creative way to refine your goals further. They help you get specific and visualise what it would be like when you get to the end of the rainbow and achieve the goals you are working on. They work regardless of the type of goal you have. You can do a vision board about the home you want to own. Or you might do a vision board to get out of debt. To help visualise these goals, find images that bring them to life. I go through magazines, Pinterest, and other websites.

For example, if you have a goal to own your own home, where is this home located? What does this home look like? Is it timber or brick? Low set or two stories? Modern or country cottage?

If you have a goal to get out of debt, what would that feel like? What would that look like? What would you be able to do if you were out of debt?

It's time to get creative. First, get a poster-sized board, art supplies, and magazines from which to get images. I also find images I can print on Pinterest and other websites and add these to my board to help me visualise my goal.

Here is my example. In 2020, I suffered a knee injury that meant I could no longer run. Even walking was painful, so my physical activity was limited. I had to wear a knee brace to work standing up, and as soon as I stopped working, I had to spend the rest of the day on the couch. By 2022, I had put on ten kilograms. My goal was to lose ten kilograms. I started a vision board to visualise the goal and motivate myself.

On my vision board, I included images of clothing I wanted to fit into again, pictures of people with a healthy weight, and even some photographs of myself before the weight gain. I had pictures of people being active and playing sports. I put my vision board on my office wall so I could see it every day. It motivated me to keep to my plan. I would see the board and not eat that snack I was thinking of. I would go for that walk in the morning, knowing it would bring me closer to that vision. It worked. Within twelve months, I had lost the ten kilograms I put on while recovering from my knee injury.

As I have three yearly goals, I have up to three vision boards on the go at any time. My yearly goals are sometimes goals leading towards my five-year goal. I had a five-year goal to build an investment portfolio to allow me to retire without waiting until I could draw a pension. To achieve this five-year goal, I had a one-year goal leading towards this goal. So, my one-year and five-year financial goals had the same vision board. It had retirement-type images, like gardening, picnic baskets on blankets under the trees, tables spread with food, and a list of books I wanted to read.

To-Dos for Week Fifteen:

1. Gather your supplies: poster boards, art supplies, and a pile of magazines. You can usually get cheap magazines at Goodwill stores.
2. Create a vision board for your yearly and five-year goals.
3. Get them onto the wall somewhere you will see them daily.

End of Week Fifteen Review

This is a fun week, and while it may seem frivolous to some, there is no doubt in my mind that visualising can help you achieve your goals. At the end of week fifteen, you have created vision boards for your selected goals and hung them on the wall where you can see them daily. For me, that is in my office. I have had people tell me they put their vision boards on their fridges or in their bathrooms. The point is to see them every day and visualise achieving the goals you have set for yourself.

WEEK SIXTEEN: WORKING OUT YOUR NET WORTH

In step eleven, setting a food budget, we touched on money for the first time. We have all heard that money can't buy you happiness, and I agree. But it is also true that being in financial trouble brings misery. In a business, there are basic financial reports that you look at regularly to see how the company is doing. Is it viable? Do we need to change anything? Are we on track to meet our goals? Without these reports, you are flying blind and, as a result, will probably crash. Do you have a financial report for your life? Most people don't, and it is a big mistake.

The standard financial reports for a business are:

- Profit and Loss
- Balance Sheet
- A budget
- Cash Flow Statement

Over the next few weeks, we will start putting together financials for your life, starting with a balance sheet or what I like to call a net worth statement. A net worth statement is a list of all of your assets and liabilities. Your net worth results from deducting all your liabilities from your assets. This result can be either positive or negative.

For example, if the only asset you have is $1,000 in the bank, but you have a credit card debt of $800, your net worth is $200 ($1,000 - $800 = $200). However, if you have $1,000 in the bank and a credit card debt of $1,500, your net worth is -$500, which is a negative amount. ($1,000 - $1,500 = -$500).

A net worth statement is a statement of your net worth at a particular point in time. First, list all your assets. This will include money in the bank, savings, investments, retirement funds, cars, and houses. The value of items is what would be a fair market value. For a car, that would be what it will sell for, not what you think it's worth because of how much you paid for it. Next, list liabilities, which are everything you owe. This includes credit card debt, car loans, the mortgage on your house, and any other amounts you owe to anybody, including student loans and tax debts. Have a look at the example below.

WEEK SIXTEEN: WORKING OUT YOUR NET WORTH

ASSET	Amount on 31 March 2024
Transaction account	$200
Savings account	$1,000
Retirement account (superannuation in Australia)	$25,000
Car	$7,500
House	$480,000
Total Assets	**$513,700**
LIABILITIES	
Credit card	$3,400
Car loan	$1,750
Mortgage	$357,200
Student loan	$30,000
Total Liabilities	**$392,350**
Net Worth (Assets minus Liabilities)	**$121,350**

This example has a positive result, but this is only sometimes the case. Imagine this person without a house or mortgage, as shown in the example below, and the result is very different. It reduced the person's net worth by leaving them with a negative net worth of -$1,450.

ASSET	Amount on 31 March 2024
Transaction account	$200
Savings account	$1,000
Retirement account (superannuation in Australia)	$25,000
Car	$7,500
Total Assets	**$33,700**
LIABILITIES	
Credit card	$3,400
Car loan	$1,750
Student loan	$30,000
Total Liabilities	**$35,150**
Net Worth (Assets minus Liabilities)	**$-1,450**

To have a wonderful life, you need to be financially secure. Money is a means of exchange. It can function like energy, allowing you to go places, do things, and have things and experiences. You need to know your net worth. You must know where you are starting from to get where you want to go. You might have a retirement goal or plan to spend big on a world tour. You must set a goal no matter what you want; to get to that goal, you must know where the starting line is. You can't get from A to B if you don't know where A is. From a financial point of view, your net worth is your starting point. You can plan to get where you want to go only once you know your starting point.

To-Dos for Week Sixteen:

1. Pick a date for your net worth statement. Each amount you add will be as of that date.
2. Gather up all your bank and other statements and list your cash-type assets.
3. Add non-cash assets, such as your house and a car, calculated at fair market value. Most of this information will be available online.
4. Gather all your debt statements, mortgage, car loans, student loans, and credit card statements.
5. List all your liabilities.
6. Subtract your total liabilities from your total assets. This is your net worth.
7. Update this once a month to see how you are progressing.
8. Make an Excel spreadsheet and record your net worth once a month. Use the graphing function so you have a visual.

End of Week Sixteen Review

This week may have been confronting for you as you saw how far you must go to get where you want to be. For others, it may have been a pleasant surprise. In either case, knowing where you are starting from is essential. Now that you do, you are ready to take the next step, building upon your achievements.

WEEK SEVENTEEN: CREATING YOUR PERSONAL INCOME AND EXPENDITURE STATEMENT

Now, it is time to look at your spending habits. A personal income and expenditure statement is a statement of income and expenses after the fact. You will need to gather information on all the bills you pay and how much you spend on everything. Review credit card statements and look at your bank accounts. This will be easy if you use a personal accounting software. If not, don't worry. You can still calculate this information.

Once you have entered all the information in either the weekly, monthly, or yearly column, you must convert monthly and annual amounts to weekly amounts. Some items are weekly expenses, such as rent or the trip to the grocery store. Other costs are monthly, like your phone bill or health insurance. Other things are yearly, like car registration. Collect all the information and add it to the income and expenditure statement.

Remember, this is recording what is happening and what you are spending, not what you wish you were spending. Don't cheat because if you do, you are only cheating yourself. You will get the most out of this exercise if you are brutally honest with yourself.

To convert the amounts from monthly to weekly, multiply them by 12 and divide by 52. In this example, I am converting a monthly health insurance amount of $380 to a weekly amount: ($380 x 12 months) / 52 weeks = $87.69 per week. I suggest you use an Excel spreadsheet to help with these calculations.

For the purpose of this book, the personal income and expenditure statement does not consider the principal paid off on a mortgage differently than the interest. It counts the full payment as an expense. For example, if your mortgage payment is $2000. and this is made up of principle and interest, technically, only the interest is an expense. The principle is not an expense as it is reducing a liability. Counting the principle and interest is more like a cash flow statement. So, by getting you to count the principle and interest what I am having you create is a hybrid between a profit and loss and a cash flow statement. Read this report together with your monthly net worth report to get a complete picture of your progress.

Example Personal Income and Expenditure Statement

WEEK SEVENTEEN CREATING YOUR PERSONAL INCOME AND EXPENDITURE STATEMENT

	Weekly	Monthly	Yearly
Income			
Gross wages	$1,000	$4,333.33	$52,000.00
Other income			
Total Income	$1,000		
Expenses			
Tax withheld	$162		
Food	$175		
Rent/mortgage	$350		
Home and contents insurance	$23		$1,200.00
Electricity	$200		
Phone and internet	$80		
Mobile phone	$40		
Car insurance	$15		$800.00
Car registration	$15		$800.00
Car fuel	$50		
Car maintenance	$19.		$1,000.00
Health insurance	$87	$380.00	
Clothing allowance	$50		
Entertainment	$100		
Credit card payment	$250		
Total Expenses	$1,616		

This is a shocking but not uncommon result. How does this happen? It's easy; people charge things that they cannot afford on credit cards. This worsens things in the long run as they must increase their credit limit or get more credit cards.

According to the Reserve Bank of Australia,[6]

- The average credit card debt in Australia is about $3,000 AUD per person.
- The average American household has over $9,000 USD in credit card debt.
- Each UK household has an average credit card debt of £2,290 GBP

This may have been another painful exercise, but once again, you must know where you are before getting to where you want to be. Knowing is half the battle. Now that you know, you can do something about it. If your result was positive, that's great. You are further down the path of being able to take that surplus and make your dreams come true with it.

To-Dos for Week Seventeen:

1. Gather your pay slips, bank statements, credit card statements, and bills.
2. Construct a personal income and expenditure statement.
3. Alternatively, if you use personal accounting software, you should be able to generate a report of your income and expenses.

4. If you had to do a reconstruction, start using software to track your income and expenses.

This was a tough week for some, but this was a vital step you needed to take to get your life on track. You might be having trouble with your income and expenses, but now that you know it, you can fix it. Now that you know how much surplus you have, you can plan to use it in the best possible way to move you towards the amazing life you have always wanted. You might be making more than you spend. Either way, getting serious about money and running your finances like a business will make a difference in your long-term financial outlook.

End of Week Seventeen Review

Please review all the previous steps and ensure you haven't let any of them slide. Remember, you are building a pyramid to success. If you let the foundational pieces fall out, it could all collapse. There is no point in fixing your finances if you are not eating and sleeping well or staying fit. You won't be around to enjoy that financial freedom.

WEEK EIGHTEEN: CREATE A BUDGET

Another essential financial tool for a business is a budget. All companies have a budget. Every year, the government releases a budget for the upcoming year. You need to do the same to run your life like a business.

A budget is a statement of all income coming in and all expenses going out, as planned for the future. This is not the same as a personal income and expenditure statement, which is after the fact.

With a budget, you begin to exert some control over the inflows and outflows of money in your life to get the results you want. Making a budget is relatively easy if you have already created a personal income and expenditure statement showing what has been happening to your money.

If your income was less than your expenses, you must take the personal income and expenditure statement you created and based on that document, either increase your income, reduce your spending, or both.

What are you doing with the surplus if your income exceeds your expenses? Without a plan, it will all just evaporate into the ether. You need to create an "expense" where you spend that money on an asset that pays you back. Let's start with where I find most people to be: their expenses are higher than their income.

Take the personal income and expenditure statement you created in week seventeen and see where you are spending on items you can reduce. Below, I have removed the monthly and yearly columns and replaced them with budget columns and comments. Let's see what we can do for this person.

Example Personal Income and Expenditure Statement versus Budget

	Weekly (the past)	Weekly Budget (the future)	Comments
Income			
Gross wages	$1,000	$1,000	
Other income			
Total Income	$1,000	$1,000	
Expenses			
Tax withheld	$162	$162	Taxes cannot be changed.
Food	$175	$100	Mindful meal planning can bring this down.
Rent/mortgage	$350	$175	If you are single and living in a house, get a housemate.

Home and contents insurance	$23	$23	Get on the phone and negotiate a better deal. Call the competition. Make sure you are getting the best possible price.
Electricity	$200	$100	Get on the phone and negotiate a better deal. Call the competition. Make sure you are getting the best possible price. A housemate can help with this as well.
Phone and internet	$80	$55	Get on the phone and negotiate a better deal. Call the competition. Make sure you are getting the best possible price.
Mobile phone	$40	$30	Get on the phone and negotiate a better deal. Call the competition. Make sure you are getting the best possible price.
Car payment			
Car insurance	$15	$15	Get on the phone and negotiate a better deal. Call the competition. Make sure you are getting the best possible price.
Car registration	$15	$15	
Car fuel	$50	$50	

Car maintenance	$19	$19	
Health insurance	$87	$80	Get on the phone and negotiate a better deal. Call the competition. Make sure you are getting the best possible price.
Clothing allowance	$50	$0	Cut the new clothes for a while. Get on your feet financially.
Entertainment	$100	$0	Cut the entertainment budget for a while. Do free things.
Credit card payment	$250	$150	Even if you have to reduce this payment, make sure it is at least the minimum payment.
Total Expenses	**$1,616**	**$974**	

In the above example, we had a person living way beyond their means, and drastic change was needed. Cutting clothing and entertainment for a while to pay off the credit cards is relatively easy. Getting a housemate is a big step, but with the current housing crisis, plenty of great people are looking for a home to share.

No matter how far out of balance in the wrong direction you are, if you start cutting your expenses, you will get closer to breaking even and eventually get to parity. Reducing the amount you are going in the red by every week is better than doing nothing. You created a net worth statement in step sixteen, which you should update regularly.

Review this with your income and expenditure statement that you created and then turned into your budget.

The other part of this equation is income. This person needs to make more money. The first thing that you can do is ask for a raise. They could also start a side hustle. The bottom line is that they need to make more money. We will cover asking for a raise and creating a side hustle later.

To-Dos for Week Eighteen:

1. Create a budget that allows you to live within your means.

This was another tough week for many. Some people see a budget as restricting their lives. I see a budget as a tool to liberate me as it makes me financially free. Having a budget is a vital step to a successful life. No business would be without one, so no person should live without one.

End of Week Eighteen Review

You have done some heavy lifting over the past few weeks. While finances are not sexy, they are vitally important to your ability to manage your life. No business would be without these basic financial reports; you should not be either. I have a business meeting with myself once a month, with my financial reports, to see how I am doing financially. I assess whether I need to make any changes or investment decisions. These last few weeks are essential steps to run your life like a business and get the desired results.

WEEK NINETEEN: HIGH-INTEREST ACCOUNTS AND NO-FEE CREDIT CARDS

You have begun to get in control of your money. You now know where your money has been going in the past. You also have a plan in place as to where your money will go in the future. Banks and financial institutions cost you money or make you money through the interest you pay or earn. As part of your financial plan, you should use these services to maximise your profit, not the banks.

Interest Coming In

Do you have an interest-bearing savings account? If so, do you know how much interest is paid on the money you have in that account? Many people have no idea of the interest rate paid by a bank on any savings they have. As interest can be a part of your income, you must get the best interest rate possible and have as much money as you can, earning interest on any given day.

Most banks have transaction accounts that are linked to savings accounts. The transaction accounts usually don't pay interest, but the savings accounts do. Your pay is usually directly deposited into your transaction account. You then pay your bills and expenses from this account.

Once you have a budget and a calendar that lets you know when bills are due, you can start transferring money to the savings account and setting this money aside for future bills you know will be due and when. This removes the money from your transaction account and stops that money from being available for "spending" on other unplanned items. In addition to keeping this money set aside for bills, that money makes you more money because it earns interest.

How much interest are you currently earning on money in your savings account? The interest rates paid by different banks vary widely. You need to shop around and get the best rate you can. As I write this book, based on an internet search, I can get as little as .05% up to 5.5% on my savings. Why would I put my money in an account and earn .05% when I could earn 5.5%? Do your homework.

Interest Going Out

Credit card interest can be very high, making purchases even more expensive. You want to get the lowest rate of interest on a credit card that you can. My top tips would be:

- Don't purchase items with a credit card. If you can't afford it, don't buy it.
- If you have to buy things on a credit card, know the credit card interest rate and get the lowest rate possible.
- Pay off your balance in full at the end of the month and take advantage of any interest-free period.

If you have credit card debt, the interest is already a problem. Look for zero-interest balance transfers, transfer the balance to that card, and eliminate the high-interest cards. This only works if you cancel the high-interest cards and do not add another card with which you can get into more debt. Most of these cards with a zero-interest rate move to a higher and sometimes very high interest rate after a honeymoon period. My current zero-interest card goes to a high interest after eighteen months. That is a long time to have a zero-interest rate. I placed a reminder on my calendar to change to another zero-interest deal a few weeks before the eighteen-month anniversary of getting that card.

Even if I have credit card debt, with no-interest balance transfers and keeping track of the honeymoon period to change to another no-interest card, I will never pay credit card interest again. Why do companies offer these deals? They rely on you to forget all about the higher interest charges in the future. They are banking on you continuing to spend money on this card after the interest rate goes up and not taking the time to make the call to save that money. They are banking on your complacency. They are making millions of dollars from people who do not have a plan.

To-Dos for Week Nineteen:

1. Find a transaction account linked to a savings account with a high interest rate and move your accounts to this bank.
2. Transfer money you do not need for this week's transactions from the transaction account to the savings account, earning interest on that money.

3. Find out what interest rate you are paying on your credit cards. Do they have any interest-free options when paying off the balance in full?

4. Find a zero-interest rate card so you can do a balance transfer.

5. Close the high-interest account so you don't charge more, increasing your debt.

6. Put a reminder on your calendar two weeks before the honeymoon period expires on the new card and the interest rate jumps up.

7. Work on paying off the balance, and don't charge any more on the card.

End of Week Nineteen Review

This week, you will make a few calls and spend time online looking for the best deal. In most cases, applications can be done online in just a few minutes. It might seem like a small step, but remember, all these steps are cumulative.

WEEK TWENTY: GET PAID WHAT YOU ARE WORTH, ASK FOR A RAISE, AND INCREASE YOUR PRICES

We have reviewed your income and expenses, created a budget, and cut your spending to ensure you live within your means. You have a bank account earning you as much interest as possible, a credit card with a low or even zero interest rate, and a plan to keep it that way. Now, we need to talk about making more money.

Most people are employed by someone else. This being the case, the number one way people make money is through a wage. If you need to make more money, you either need to get paid more in the job you already have or move to a new job that will pay you more.

Getting Paid More at Your Current Job

How much are you getting paid? Is the wage you are earning reasonable within industry standards? Are you getting paid what you are worth? These are all excellent questions and things you need to discover. There are websites where you can find this information.

Let's say you are a librarian in Queensland, earning $75,000 annually. I typed "average pay for a librarian" into Google and found this information on Seek: The average pay range for a librarian in Queensland was $80,000 to $90,000.

Armed with this information, you should ask for a raise of between $5,000 and $15,000, depending on your experience and position within the library system. Not asking for a raise is a major factor in not getting the raise you want or deserve. This is a bigger problem with women than it is with men. Men tend to overestimate their value as employees, while women tend to underestimate their value as employees.

Changing Jobs to Get Better Pay

What if you have tried to get better pay at your current job but didn't get the raise you sought? You could change jobs. Let's use the librarian example again. Councils run libraries, and in Southeast Queensland, there are several. You could work in a library run by the Brisbane City Council, Logan City Council, or Redland City Council, to mention a few. Do they all pay the same for their librarians? Employers compete with each other for talent when there are staff shortages. It is all about supply and demand.

While still employed as a librarian for one council, which has yet to give you the raise you requested, you can start looking at and applying for positions available at another council for similar jobs. Are they hiring? Are they offering more money? Would you have to travel more, and if so, would the increased pay offered be worth it? Economic times change. Sometimes, it is an employer's market; other times, it is an employee's market. Don't blow your job if there isn't a better one out there. But don't assume there isn't something better out there without looking.

Raising Your Prices

Self-employed people can also ask for a raise, which comes as a price increase. Knowing when and how much you can raise your prices takes a bit of research. You must determine what other people in your industry charge for similar services. You might find out that you are charging significantly less than others. While this might generate lots of work, you work harder for less money. Increasing your prices might cause you to lose a few customers, but what if you earned the same money but for less work, at the same time as lowering your expenses?

I am a writer and public speaker. Most of my teaching and public speaking work occurs later in the week and on the weekend, so I write early in the week and speak later in the week. Most people want a Saturday, and there are only fifty-two a year, so supply is limited. Much of my work comes from speaking in libraries, and I am so grateful for this support as a writer. I get a speaker fee and sell my books. This helps me afford to stay home and work on my next book. One council continuously asked me to speak at libraries for free, while others paid me a fee. As a newly published writer, I took every gig I could get, paid or not, hoping to sell a book or two after the event.

As my writing became more well-known, I received more invitations to speak, both paid and unpaid. It was getting to the point that I was working seven days a week, including several evenings. It was physically, mentally, and financially unsustainable. I was then given life-changing advice from my brother, who had previously worked as an entertainer. He told me that if I agreed to work for nothing, I let people know I was worth nothing. He told me to work out reasonable prices for my time and effort, including the expenses of getting to my event. I created a list of my services and set prices for each.

As calls and emails came in requesting that I come and give a demonstration or lecture, I politely said yes and gave them my price. I was amazed that the response was so positive. I thought my bookings would go down, but the opposite occurred. Bookings increased. I had let people know I was not free and I was not cheap; I was valuable. One council never booked me again as they did not wish to pay me. However, this worked out well for me as I had so many bookings and had no time to work for them for free.

I now increase my prices every year, keeping pace with cost increases. Whenever I become overwhelmed with work, I increase my prices based on supply and demand. The people who value my services are happy to pay me. The people who do not value my services fall by the wayside. Why would you want to work with someone who did not value you?

Look at it this way. Say you have a service you can deliver in a week. You have fifty-two weeks a year. You intend to work fifty of those weeks. That means you can sell fifty of these services in a year. You charge $1,000 for the service, which gives you $50,000 annual income potential.

If you increase your prices to $1,100 per service, you get $55,000 for the same amount of work. You have made the right decision if you can sell fifty each year at this price. If you sell more than you can deliver and have to put people on a waiting list, you probably need to charge more. What if you charge $1,500 for this same service but could only sell forty-eight each year? You are now making $72,000 a year and get an extra two weeks off.

Some people will be in a saturated industry. They must keep their prices the same as there is too much competition. Rising prices will cause them to lose customers to the point of not having enough work to be viable.

For example, what if you are a self-employed hairdresser? You are in a town on the main street with six other hairdressers. You are all competing for a limited number of customers. A part of this competition has become price cutting. To stay in business, you need to work harder for less money. This is not a recipe for success. What do you do?

- You might need to get out of this industry.
- You might choose to stay in the industry but go to a less saturated area.
- You might have to change your business by adding other products and services that set you apart from the competition.

If you find yourself in this situation, I recommend you read *Blue Ocean Strategy, How to Create Uncontested Market Space and Make Competition Irrelevant*, by W. C. Kim and R. Mauborgne. It has some big ideas you can apply to your little piece of the pie. It discusses industry disrupters like Netflix, who put video stores like Blockbuster out of business or forced them to change significantly.[7] It's about thinking outside the box and could help you distinguish yourself from the competition.

Let's go back to the hairdresser example. You cannot compete on price without working harder for less money, so don't. Compete on a service that sets you apart. Add other beauty services. Be that place where you can get a haircut and colour, a facial, have your nails done, have a colour consultation so you wear the right colours for your skin tone, hair, and eye colour, and get a fashion consultation. You can swim with the sharks (red ocean) and try to compete in a saturated market, or you can swim in the blue ocean and do something no one else is doing.

To-Dos for Week Twenty:

1. If you are employed, find out the market rate for your job. Are you on par, below, or above the going rate?
2. With the information gained in step one, negotiate a better pay packet.
3. If step two went well, you are done. If not, look at other employers that could hire you and consider moving to one of those employers.
4. While still employed, apply for better-paying positions advertised in your area.

If you are self-employed:

1. Compare your prices and fees to others in the same industry. How do they compare?
2. Increase your prices with the information you gained from step one.
3. Increase your prices if you have more work than you can handle.

4. If you do not have enough work and increasing your prices is impossible, you must consider whether being self-employed in your industry is viable.

5. Read *Blue Ocean Strategy, How to Create Uncontested Market Space and Make Competition Irrelevant*.

6. You might need to change industries or locations or find ways to differentiate your business from the competition.

End of Week Twenty Review

Many of us have our identity closely tied to our occupation. Thinking of asking for a raise might be scary, but the worst that can happen is that the boss says no. Changing jobs is a bigger deal as we get used to where we are and who we work with. Changing jobs comes with some risks as well.

Changing businesses, locations, or industries as a self-employed person can be daunting, but staying in a business that doesn't make you enough money just because change is scary is not a good idea. I co-founded Green Living Australia in 2004. It has changed directions several times in the last twenty years, introducing new product lines, phasing out older ones, having physical locations, and eventually moving solely online. My company had to change with the times and adapt to competitors coming into the market. If you are successful, someone will copy you. Keep innovating and stand out from the crowd.

WEEK TWENTY-ONE: INSURANCE

Insurance is one of those things you buy that you hope you will never need to use. It seems counterintuitive. There is nothing else I have ever purchased that I wish I would never need. And when I did need it, I was so grateful to have it. For those who purchased insurance and never needed it, what they bought was peace of mind.

You can plan a great life, work hard, and make all your dreams come true, but it can all be wiped out instantly by an accident, a storm, or a fire. Bad things happen to good people all the time. Insurance needs to be a part of your plan. You need to protect what you have.

Health Insurance

Health insurance is an essential part of your plan. Accidents, injuries, and illnesses can affect anyone at any time. What type of health insurance you have will be based on your individual needs, and you may want to seek professional advice on this. I went with hospital coverage. I figured I could afford trips to the general practitioner, but if I needed more significant care and I was hospitalised, I would want a private room. Hospital coverage was essential from my point of view.

Investigate your health insurance options and get the best coverage you can afford. Remember, it has to go into your budget. As you improve your financial position, you may upgrade your coverage. I review my coverage once a year.

If you cannot afford health insurance now and you are in Australia, Canada, or the UK, you are lucky to have access to the public health system. You could leave health insurance out for a while until you have the rest of your finances under control but get it as soon as possible. If you are in America, you need to prioritise health coverage as the cost of medical treatment is very high, and there is little or no help from the government.

Home and Contents Insurance

If you own a home, it is probably your largest asset and needs protection. Even if you rent, you should still have contents insurance. Investigate different companies and find the best home and contents insurance deal. This does not necessarily mean the cheapest. Some insurers are better than others, so consider service ratings and price. I selected a middle-of-the-range price from an insurer that had great service reviews. I wanted affordable insurance but with a company with a reputation for promptly paying claims. It is no good to have insurance that does not pay and then have to get legal assistance with your claim.

I paid home and contents insurance for years and never made a claim. Then, one day, I got a call when I was away from home for work, telling me there had been a fire at my home. While the house did not burn, another building on my property did, and it was destroyed, along with everything in it. The insurance company immediately paid me for the contents and took care of everything regarding the rebuild. They even built it back better.

The cost of the contents and the rebuild far exceeded all that I had ever paid this insurance company, and without this insurance, I would not be in the same financial position I am in today. Having an insurance company project manage the rebuild was a stress-free event for me. I did not have to worry about hiring tradies or working with the local council on approvals. When bad things happen, you need help, and a good insurance policy with a reputable company makes a big difference.

Motor Vehicle Insurance

After a house, a car can be your next biggest asset. Being on the roads can be dangerous. You may cause an accident, in which case you are responsible for damaging your car and the other person's property. Or you could be the victim in a car accident due to someone else's mistake. What if that person doesn't have insurance and can't pay for your damages?

As a teacher and public speaker, I travel for work and spend a lot of time behind the wheel. You don't have to do anything wrong to be in an accident. No one plans to have an accident, and it can happen to anyone. If you don't have insurance, you might be unable to fix or replace your car.

There are different levels of coverage with various options. Find out what would be best for you, considering your financial position, your car's value, and your location. For example, if you drive a new car, having a policy that covers your car and liability for someone else's car might be what you need. However, if you are driving a very low-value vehicle, you might opt for just liability coverage because your car has little value, so why insure it? I live in the country with dirt roads, so I wanted to add windshield coverage based on my location. Talk to a professional about your motor vehicle insurance needs.

Life Insurance

Life insurance can also be an essential part of your life plan. Then again, you might not think it necessary. This one depends more on your age and stage of life. I no longer have life insurance, but I did in the past. My purpose in having life insurance was to protect my children. When I had children living at home, going to school, and depending on me financially, life insurance was necessary. I needed to ensure my children would be financially secure if anything happened to me. If you have people depending on you, life insurance must be considered.

My children are all grown now, the mortgage is paid, and I am financially independent. Based on my age, stage of life, and financial situation, I no longer see the value of life insurance, so I no longer have it.

Income Insurance

Another kind of insurance that may be applicable to your situation is income insurance. If you are self-employed and you are injured, how would you make money, pay your bills, and put food on the table? If you work for someone else but got sick and could not work, what would you do? A financial disaster is just a few pay cheques away for many people. Look into income insurance, which is often available through your superannuation.

To-Dos for Week Twenty-One:

1. Investigate health, auto, home, contents, income, and life insurance.
2. Obtain the appropriate insurance for your situation and add it to your budget. Don't add things you can't afford. Remember, you have to live within your means.
3. Add your insurance to your budget.
4. Add a yearly review to your calendar.

End of Week Twenty-One Review

In this section, I am not saying you should have any particular type of insurance but that you should investigate and determine what insurance you need to protect yourself and your loved ones. I advise getting an insurance broker or a professional and working out the insurance you need for your life. Your insurance plan will be different from someone else's. I now have health, home and contents, and car insurance, but no life or income insurance. That works for me, but maybe not for you. When I had younger children, I had home and contents, car insurance, life insurance and income protection. I could not afford health insurance and had to rely on the public health system. I was thankful to live in Australia, where a public health system was available, making my insurance plan workable.

WEEK TWENTY-TWO: YOU AND THE TAXMAN

Benjamin Franklin said, "…in this world, nothing can be said to be certain, except death and taxes." [8]

That was a long time ago, but nothing much has changed. You will have to file and pay taxes. The trick is to pay all that you owe and no more and to make it as painless administratively as possible. I don't mind paying my share of taxes. What I don't like is the hours and hours it takes to document and keep track of money so that my taxes can be filed correctly. I am not an accountant or a tax lawyer, so I prefer to hire a qualified professional to do this type of work for me.

As a business owner, I think this is an excellent solution, but it might not be necessary for everyone. If you are an employee, have no other business activity, and don't buy and sell assets (real estate, company shares, bonds, etc.), you might not need an accountant and can do a simple return once a year online. But when things get complicated, a good accountant is a great person to have on your team.

I am great at what I do, and you are probably great at what you do. I am not great at being an accountant. Over the years, I have learned that hiring professionals to do things I am not an expert in saves me time and money in the long run. Not only can a good accountant ensure that your taxes are filed correctly and on time, but they can also help you plan your finances for the following year to take advantage of tax law best, lowering your tax bill. You can get advice on making additional contributions to superannuation to reduce your tax bill and save for retirement. If you are in business and need a new company car, should you buy or lease, and how will that affect your taxes? Ask your accountant. A good accountant doesn't just file taxes for you after the fact. They help you have a better financial future by advising on strategies to reduce your tax liability in the next year based on ever-changing tax laws and their interpretation.

You must collect information annually to present to your accountant at tax time. Make this as easy as you can for yourself. You can purchase inexpensive personal accounting software to track your income and expenses. You can also do this easily on an Excel spreadsheet. I use an accounting package for my business, but I use an Excel spreadsheet for my expenses, and I only track transactions that affect my tax liability. For example, I do not have to track what I spend on entertainment or my yearly holiday, but I do have to track donations to registered charitable organisations and investment expenses such as the fees charged for buying and selling investment instruments like exchange-traded funds (ETFs).

I also keep electronic copies of all receipts relating to the items I wish to claim. At the beginning of the tax year, I create a folder for that tax year. I have other folders for different expenses within that folder. One is called donations, while another is called investment expenses.

You can create as many subfolders as you need. Just be sure that they are all in that year's tax folder. At the end of the tax year, you can share this folder and the Excel spreadsheet with your accountant, making her job easy and saving you money. Keep on top of your paperwork. If you give your accountant a shoebox full of receipts and she has to spend time sorting it all out, you will get a bigger tax preparation bill. Accurate accounting is vital in business and your personal life.

2023/2024 Tax Year (Folder)	
Donations (Sub-folder)	Investment expenses (Sub-folder)

To-Dos for Week Twenty-Two:

1. Create an Excel spreadsheet to track your tax-deductible expenses for the year.
2. Create a folder on your computer (or physical if you prefer) to keep all that year's tax receipts.
3. Find an accountant that you are happy to add to your team.

Not everyone will do step three, and if your return is simple and you do not need an accountant, that is OK. Just be sure you are not paying more taxes than you should be. It doesn't make sense to save $200 on an accountant and lose $500 in extra tax. This is a decision you need to make based on your circumstances.

End of Week Twenty-Two Review

Taxes are a part of life. Resistance is futile. You need to pay what you owe when you owe it. You are not required to make additional contributions to the government. Don't let poor administration cost you money.

WEEK TWENTY-THREE: PAY YOURSELF FIRST

Saving money for your future is a big part of having a great life. But if you are like most people, the money comes in, and then it goes right back out again. Expenses always rise to meet income. This law is known as Parkinson's Law, one of the best-known and most important business rules.[9] If you apply this rule to your personal finances, you will see it in action; every time you increase your income, your expenses increase accordingly. There is never any money left over, so how can you ever build for the future or save for a house deposit?

The trick is to pay yourself first. You have to "spend" the money on yourself in a way that saves it for your future. Spending it into a savings account removes the money from your income, so expenses cannot rise to match. Most people are just not good at this. This is why, in Australia, the government introduced mandatory employer superannuation contributions that you, the owner of that money, cannot access. It's a great idea, and many people who would have been flat broke at retirement age now have superannuation that they can draw on.

What makes superannuation work is that the money is not in your control, which also is its greatest flaw. If something happens in your life and you need to access your superannuation, you can apply to access your money, and that application will be granted under limited circumstances. The problem is that someone else decides whether your reason is valid. As an example, if you need to access your superannuation due to a terminal medical condition, you can apply but can be denied, even if your reason is valid.

Someone I knew was in the hospital dying of cancer. They were not expected to live and would never leave the hospital. This man was in a shared ward due to a lack of funds for a private room and had no hospital insurance coverage. It would have made his remaining time much more comfortable if he could have accessed his superannuation and paid for a private room. An application to access his superannuation was made and denied. He died several weeks later, never having been able to access the superannuation he had been contributing to all his life. His family inherited his superannuation, but they would have much rather been allowed to provide better care for their loved one when he needed it.

This is just one example where I have personal knowledge. Still, a quick internet search showed me a segment in early 2024 about a terminally ill grandfather who was denied access to his superannuation.[10] There is another story about a single mom with breast cancer who was also denied.[11] What if these kinds of denials are not isolated incidents? Why do I see so many superannuation lawyers offering their services and trying to get you access to your own money when you legitimately need it? If it is a simple matter of supply and demand, there must be many people trying to access superannuation in these situations—enough to create a whole specialty within our legal community. Don't get me wrong. Superannuation is great; it's just not perfect.

Another thing that worries me about having superannuation as the only savings for the future is that the government can change the rules at any time. They can change how the money is taxed, the age at which you can access it, the reasons for early access, and the application process. Saving money for the future is important, and superannuation is a great way to do this. But control is also important. In addition to superannuation, you must set money aside for a rainy day, retirement, and large purchases, such as a home deposit.

How do you do this? You pay yourself first. When that money, usually your pay from your employer, comes into your bank account, immediately spend some on yourself as a payment into a high-interest savings account. At this point, having completed week nineteen, the only savings account you should have is a high-interest savings account. If you pay yourself first and remove that money from your transaction account, you force yourself to live on the rest, limiting the growth of your expenses.

The book *The Richest Man in Babylon* recommends saving a portion of one's income before any other expenses.[12] A good place to start is 10% to 15%. To make this even easier for you, you can set this up as an automatic transfer. It's a set-and-forget savings plan.

I have a transaction account where my income comes in every Friday, and I have an automatic transfer set up for every Monday. This time works for me as I work most weekends, so I don't spend money over the weekend on the usual leisure activities. By Monday, the money is gone from my account, so I don't spend it from my transaction account when shopping or paying bills. Set whatever day works for you, but an automated savings plan is a great way to ensure you never spend that money.

Remember, there will always be more things to spend your money on. The advertising industry focuses on making you think you need things you don't and trying to take your hard-earned money out of your pocket and into their clients' pockets. It's their job, and they are great at it. I am deciding for myself where to spend that money. First, it gets paid into a savings account. From there, I can choose how to spend it on assets that will appreciate over time, not on things that are worth next to nothing the moment I purchase them.

To-Dos for Week Twenty-Three:

- Read the book *The Richest Man in Babylon*.
- Decide what percentage you will set aside for yourself every week, fortnightly, or monthly, depending on when you get paid.
- Set up an automatic transfer to "spend" this amount on yourself and put it into your savings account.
- Don't touch this money. It is yours. Don't give it away because of someone's edgy advertising.

End of Week Twenty-Three Review

Paying yourself first is a three-thousand-year-old idea; if we do it, there will be a fundamental shift in the quality of our lives. It's what wealthy people have been doing for centuries and what poor people don't do. So, what do you want to be, rich or poor? As unbelievable as it might sound, the choice is yours, and we make that choice every day.

WEEK TWENTY-FOUR: PLAY THE FRUGAL GAME

You have created a budget, and you are paying yourself first. You have focused on getting a raise to increase your income, but you can do more. You can improve your savings by playing the frugal game. Saving money seems like a burden to most people. It makes you think of going without. But rich people didn't get rich by spending; they got rich by saving and investing. I don't want to work forever. Instead of trading my hours for money, I want my money to work for me. So, I carefully think about where I spend my money, which makes me frugal.

In the book *The Millionaire Next Door: The Surprising Secrets of America's Wealthy* by Thomas J. Stanley and William D. Danko, it is revealed that most of the millionaires in America do not live in mansions, drive a Bentley, or stay in expensive hotels on their holidays.[13] They live ordinary lives, live in ordinary houses, and drive ordinary cars. They don't look rich; they are rich. Conversely, many people you see living in those mansions, driving fancy cars and wearing expensive designer clothes have far more liabilities than they do assets. They look rich, but they are, in fact, poor.

How often do you see stories in the news or magazines about supposedly rich people going bankrupt? These people made millions of dollars, yet, at the end of the day, they have nothing. These people felt the need to be flashy with their money and ended up with none. Real wealth is not showy. Sam Walton, the founder of Walmart, continued to drive his old pickup truck after becoming a multi-millionaire. Warren Buffet still lives in the house he purchased in 1958 for $31,500, and he is a billionaire.

The message is don't upsize as your income increases. Find ways to save money, then spend that money on assets that will eventually free you from work and allow that money to work for you. Go back and analyse your budget and spending habits. Can you cut some of your expenses? Can you take that money saved and use it to earn more money?

My cost of living is very low because I designed my life that way. It did not happen by accident. I live in the country rather than the city because I love it and because housing is much more affordable. It allowed me to pay off my mortgage faster. The council rates are also much lower than those of a city house. My power bills are either very low or non-existent because I invested in a solar power system. My clothing expenses are very low because I choose to have a few items I can put together in different ways to create outfits for every occasion. As I work from home as a writer, the basic building blocks of my wardrobe are jeans, shirts, and sweaters. I also do cooking shows on the weekend, so I add aprons to the jeans, shirts, and sweaters. If I need a fantastic dress for a special event, I do not spend a fortune on a dress I might only wear once. I borrow one or rent one for much less than the purchase price. For a black-tie charity ball, you could easily spend over $1,000 on a dress. You can rent one for a fraction of the cost.

My food bill is also low because I make a meal plan, shopping list, and food budget. I do meal prep, which we covered in weeks nine through eleven. I have a garden where I grow some of my food. I enjoy cooking, so I bake bread and make all my meals from scratch. When I travel to work on the weekends, I bring my prepared food with me. It's cheaper and healthier than eating out. Thanks to week nineteen, I never pay interest on credit cards.

One of my other passions is reading, and I do buy books. However, I have also joined a library and requested the books I want. If they are not already available in my local library, they arrive within a few days in most cases.

I don't smoke. It is an expensive and deadly habit. I have an occasional glass of wine, but other than that, I don't drink.

Do I like to spend money? Sure, I do. I want to buy assets that make me money, and I enjoy shopping for good investments.

This frugal way of life makes me happy, healthy, and wealthy. Find ways to play the frugal game and become the millionaire next door. Don't tell anyone. Just do it.

To-Dos for Week Twenty-Four:

1. Read *The Millionaire Next Door*. (Borrow it for free from your local library.)
2. Analyse your spending and budget and look for places to cut your expenses.

3. Add the resulting savings to your high-interest savings account.
4. Any time you want to purchase something, don't. Wait a few days and see if you still want that thing. It avoids impulse buys.

End of Week Twenty-Four Review

Playing the frugal game can be very rewarding. You will be in excellent company with many millionaires and billionaires. Driving a fancy car and living in a fancy house does not make you rich. Having more money than you need makes you rich. Being able to stop work any time you want to and be just fine makes you rich. Working sixty hours a week to afford material possessions to impress others is not wealth.

WEEK TWENTY-FIVE: GETTING OUT OF DEBT

Australia has some of the highest debt levels in the world. As of December 2022, the average Australian household debt was $261,492 AUD. In America, it is $104,215 USD; in the UK, it is £64,296 GBP. [14]

There seems to be a cultural crisis regarding money and material possessions. We want stuff, and we want it now, not after we have earned the money for it, but before. Debt costs money, so we effectively pay far more for our stuff than we should because we cannot wait. This was not always the case.

Not long ago, you went to work, started a business, or did whatever you did to earn money. You got paid. You could only spend what you had; if you wanted something that cost more, you saved until you had the money.

Now, you get a job and get paid. You apply for credit, which is easy to get, and you spend someone else's money. You continue to work to pay off the debt, paying interest that significantly increases the cost of what you purchased. You see something else you want, so you get more credit and pay more bills plus interest. You never have money left over to save. But you have a lot of stuff that is worth very little second-hand. As I noted in week seventeen, in 2024, Australia's average credit card debt was about $3,000 per account. Keep in mind that most people have multiple accounts.

So, how do you get out of debt? The first thing you should do is stop borrowing money. Charging stuff on a credit card is borrowing money. You are not spending your money; it is the bank's money. If you don't have the money for something, don't get it—period!

The next step is to gather all your debts, every charge account, credit card, and loan. Put them all on an Excel spreadsheet with the total balances in one column, interest rate in another column, and minimum payment in another. Sort them into descending order based on the interest rate, not the total amount due or minimum payment. What is important is the interest rate you are being charged. This is how much it costs you to borrow that money.

Ensure that you pay the minimum payment of every debt and that it is included in your budget. Once the minimum payment is made, you can focus on paying extra on your debts. In week twenty-three, we talked about paying yourself first and making this 10% to 15%. If I had debts, I would pay myself 10% and have the other 5% go towards additional payments on my cards. In addition, any extra money I saved for being frugal from week twenty-four would also go towards paying off my debts.

Whenever possible, roll the high-interest credit cards onto an interest-free card that allows for a balance transfer. However, you can only do this with some types of debt. Pay the debt with the highest interest first. It's the one costing you the most. Once that debt is paid off, move on to the next most expensive debt. When you pay off another debt, you free up more money for the next debt. You end up with a snowball effect as your debt progress accelerates from the highest interest to the lowest interest and, finally, the interest-free cards you rolled balances onto.

Warning: This will only work if you STOP spending money you do not have, which means stop using credit to buy things you can't afford.

To-Dos for Week Twenty-Five:

1. Collect all of your debt information.
2. Roll any credit cards with interest onto zero-interest cards. See week nineteen.
3. Enter your debts into a spreadsheet with total due, minimum payment, and interest rate.
4. Make the minimum payment and add them to your budget. See week eighteen.
5. Use extra cash to pay the debt with the highest interest.
6. Move to the next-highest-interest debt once the first one has been paid off.

End of Week Twenty-Five Review

Once you have paid off your debts, you will experience a sense of priceless freedom. For me, it was life-changing. How would it make you feel to be indebted to no one? It's a far better feeling than any retail therapy could ever give you, and it is worth working for. Free yourself.

WEEK TWENTY-SIX: AVOID HIGH-COST, LOW-BENEFIT DEBT

In week twenty-five, we discussed getting out of debt and the importance of not spending money you do not have. While I do not retract anything I said, there are exceptions. There is a concept of good debt versus bad debt. On the Investopedia website, it states that debt can be considered good if it has the potential to increase your net worth.[15] An example of this is when purchasing real estate. You might want to buy a house for $750,000. You can't save for the whole amount, so you get a loan. While you pay off the loan, plus interest, the property's value is increasing.

I will give you an example. I purchased two warehouses for my business for about $600,000. I have been paying the mortgage (principal and interest) out of my business's income. I have spent about the same amount on this payment as I would have paid in rent. The warehouses are now worth $1,200,000. If I had not borrowed the money for the warehouses, I would have paid rent, which would have been dead money. Because I borrowed and paid the money back, I now have a property value of $1,200,000. According to the definition on Investopedia, this was good debt.

Investopedia defines bad debt as money borrowed to purchase rapidly depreciating assets or assets for consumption.[16] An example of bad debt would be charging a holiday, new clothes, or dinner with friends on your credit card. None of these things will appreciate in value. There is no return on investment with these expenditures, and it wasn't your money; it was the banks.

I cannot give you financial advice on what good and bad debt is for you as we are all different. There are plenty of financial planners out there who could help you. I can tell you what I did and how it worked out for me. What I want you to take away this week is that there is a difference between good and bad debt and that there is no one-size-fits-all. There is clearly debt that has no return on investment, and this is the debt I want your life plan to avoid.

To-Dos for Week Twenty-Six:

1. Review your debts and determine which are good and bad debts.
2. Commit to not entering into any future bad debt. Always look at the return on investment and seek financial advice when needed.

End of Week Twenty-Six Review

Congratulations. You are now halfway through the year and this book. We have focused more on life's finances for the last three months. While it is challenging, it is vital to get this under control if you want to run your life like a business and be successful. Think about how far you have come over the last twenty-six weeks. How different is your life? Sometimes, it's hard work, but nothing worth having comes to us easily. In one year, you can transform your life, but only if you follow the path. If you made it this far, you are on the home stretch. Keep going. I promise it's worth it.

WEEK TWENTY-SEVEN: OWNING YOUR OWN HOME

Owning my own home was the best financial decision I ever made. The day I paid off my house, I popped the cork on a bottle of champagne and celebrated. I felt like the weight of the world had been lifted off my shoulders. It was mine—all mine.

Owning your home can be less stressful, as you never need to worry that the landlord will raise the rent or ask you to leave. What if the house you rent is sold and the new owner wants to move in? Home-ownership gives you more control and security. In addition to the security, real estate tends to increase in value over time, putting you in a stronger financial position than renting. When you pay rent, you are paying off someone else's mortgage.

Depending on your age and stage of life, you may already own a home, or you might still be renting. When I came home from America in 2002, I rented until I could save up for a down payment on a house. The house I could afford was at the lower end of the market, in a cheaper suburb further away from the city. It was not my dream home, but that was OK. I knew I had to enter the market as house prices continued to increase. I bought a fixer-upper, improved the property, sold it, and bought a better house.

Let's start with the person who is renting right now. You will need to save up for a down payment. In previous weeks, you created a budget and started playing the frugal game, saving by paying yourself first and paying off your debts. This is all very necessary if you want to buy a house. Banks don't loan money to people with no savings but lots of debt. To buy a home, the best position to be in is to:

- Have a good credit score (paid your bills on time in the past)
- Be debt free
- Have money in a savings account
- Have a consistent track record of savings
- Be able to show sufficient income to meet your expenses and home loan payments

All of these are covered in the activities of the previous weeks.

Once you are financially able to buy a house, start looking for one you can afford without experiencing mortgage stress if interest rates go up. This is not necessarily your forever home.

The first house I bought cost $124,000. It needed work, but at least I was no longer renting. My payments were about the same as what I would have been paying for rent, so I was happy with my decision, and it caused no financial stress. I sold this house for about $240,000.

The second house I bought cost me $185,000. It also needed work but was bigger, on a larger block, and had more potential than the first house. I sold this house for $490,000.

The third house was to be my forever home. I designed it myself with the help of an architect and worked closely with my builder to get just the outcome I wanted. It was situated on twelve acres in the country and was perfect. I still live there today. It is indeed my forever home.

If I had not bought that first home, in a cheaper suburb, with terrible ugly shag carpet that had not been updated since the seventies, an outdated kitchen and bathroom, and in need of a paint job, I would not have my dream home today. Don't expect your first home to be the home of your dreams.

I know people who bought an apartment when that was not what they wanted permanently. They were renting an apartment and saving for a house, and the prices were going up so fast they couldn't save for a house deposit. They could, however, get a deposit for an apartment that was cheaper than a house. When the opportunity came up to buy the apartment they were living in, they jumped at the chance. They continued to save at the same rate, but they also got to benefit from the increasing value of the apartment. Within two years, they could sell the apartment and buy a house.

What if you already own a home? That's great, but do you own it, or does the bank? I want you to have that cork-popping moment when you pay off that house. Your mortgage is a debt, so it should be on that list you made in week twenty-five. It will probably be at the bottom of the list with the lowest interest rate. You are working from the top down, paying off those high-interest-rate debts first because that debt costs you more. Once those debts are paid off, you can start to make extra payments on the home. In theory, this is a great idea. The trouble is that different loans have different rules, so getting financial advice here would be essential.

I would consider a home loan good debt, as it is for an appreciating asset. If you can't make extra payments on your home loan because it is on a fixed rate and additional payments are not within the loan agreement, don't panic; it's good debt. Every fixed-rate loan comes to an end one day. Once that happens and you revert to a variable rate, it's time to negotiate a better deal for yourself and pay off a chunk of the balance if you can.

I have been paying a mortgage on two warehouses for my business, and the loan has been paid at a fixed rate for the past three years. I could not make extra payments during the fixed-rate term, which ended in April 2024, during a high-interest-rate cycle. My loan immediately jumped to 8.25%. I did four things right away.

- I called the bank and asked for a better deal.
- I called other banks to see if they could do even better.
- I signed a new contract for a lower, but still high, variable rate. The fixed rates offered were not reasonable.
- I started making extra payments every month.

My loan was cheap, but now it is expensive, so I want to get rid of it as fast as possible. I will keep my eye on the interest rates and fix it again if that is appropriate, but for now, I will smash out the extra payments and pay it off.

Homeownership is a part of the Great Australian Dream. It is a symbol of financial success and independence. Insecure housing is a major problem that endangers people physically and mentally. Renting might not be considered insecure housing according to the definition. Still, a landlord can always increase the rent, sell the property, or refuse to renew your lease for another reason. It is not your house. And if it is not your house, how secure is it really?

To-Dos for Week Twenty-Seven:

If you are renting:

1. By working on weeks twenty-three, twenty-four, and twenty-five, make yourself a safe bet for a bank to loan you money.
2. Save for a deposit.
3. Look for your first home. This does not have to be your forever home, but one you can afford.

If you own a home:

1. Make sure you have the best loan you can get and be willing to change banks to get it.
2. After doing weeks twenty-three, twenty-four, and twenty-five, make extra payments on your home loan if you can.
3. Keep your home well-maintained to increase its value.

End of Week Twenty-Seven Review

This is a big step, and while you cannot buy or pay off a house in a week, you can plan how to get there and get started.

WEEK TWENTY-EIGHT: INVESTING FOR THE LONG HALL

You are doing well. I know you have a lot going on, but you have a plan, and you are organised. You have worked hard to get where you are. Now it is time for your money to start working for you rather than you working for your money.

In Australia, we have superannuation, which our employers pay for us. This builds us a nest egg for retirement, which is brilliant. While the rules change occasionally, putting additional money into superannuation can increase your retirement savings and reduce your taxes. You should talk to your accountant or financial planner and determine how much extra, if any, you should pay into superannuation each year. I cannot give you this kind of advice as I am not qualified. I talk to my accountant yearly to see what I can do best based on the current legislation, rules, and my financial situation. She is the expert, and I count on her advice to give me the best tax advantage. But as I discussed earlier superannuation should not be your only investment

You can also invest in:

- Stocks

- Bonds
- Real estate
- Cryptocurrency
- Commodities
- Cash
- Exchange-traded funds (ETFs)
- Mutual funds
- Corporate bonds

There are other financial instruments you can invest in, but I aim to keep it simple. I am not a financial planner. I do not think putting all your eggs in one basket is a good idea, so I have a diversified approach to my investing. In addition to my superannuation, I have the following investments:

- Stocks
- Real estate
- Cryptocurrency
- Cash
- ETFs

What you have in yours will depend on your financial situation, how much risk you are willing to take, your age, and your goals. Let's examine how I have set myself up and why.

Stocks

I am not a day trader or stock picker. I am not a short-term investor. I am in this for the long haul. I want my money to make me money

WEEK TWENTY-EIGHT: INVESTING FOR THE LONG HALL

for the rest of my life. That being said, there are a few companies that I want to invest in because I believe in them. When you buy stocks, you purchase a part of a company, so I only buy stocks in a company I would want to own. I need to understand them and care about them. This approach is not for everyone, but it works for me. I only have shares in a couple of companies.

Real Estate

I have my fully paid-off home and two warehouses to run my company out of. They have all increased significantly in value and have been excellent investments for the long haul.

Cryptocurrency

I am playing with this with a small amount of money. It still seems strange, and I do not fully understand it, but my knowledge is growing. It seems risky to me, so my investment has been small. If I lose it, I won't be too upset. As of today, I am up 53% in the last six months. Not bad.

Cash

I have some cash in high-interest accounts.

ETFs

This is where most of my investing goes, allowing me to diversify easily. ETFs are a low-cost way to earn a return similar to an index or a commodity. They can also help to diversify your investments. I select different sectors of the economy and currently have four ETFs I invest in regularly. Performance has ranged from as low as 8% to as high as 25%. I am doing well and will continue to work with the four I have chosen.

The key to good investing is:

- Go for the long haul. Time in the market, not timing is key.
- Leverage price cost averaging and be consistent.
- Get proper financial advice.

I use an investment platform and set up an automatic debit from my bank account every Monday. That money goes into my investments using instructions I have entered into my platform. This platform gives me access to the Australian and American markets. I can invest in stocks and ETFs. Their fees are low, and it has an easy-to-read dashboard I can access that gives me a great picture of how I am doing financially. I can also link my bank and superannuation accounts and enter other assets, giving me a complete picture of my financial situation. I also like it because it is Australian.

My strategy is to buy good-quality investments and hold them. I do not worry about the market's daily ups and downs; I am in this for the long haul. I have a set amount that goes into my investments every week. I buy the same selected investments regularly, regardless of their price. If a stock or ETF price goes down, I automatically purchase more for the same money. This method, also known as dollar cost averaging, can help you manage timing risk and stick to your long-term plan.

Do your research, talk to a professional, and find a platform that works for you. Choose one you can automate, set and forget, and make money while you sleep. While set-and-forget is what I was

WEEK TWENTY-EIGHT: INVESTING FOR THE LONG HALL

looking for, I log in once a month and check my progress. Because of this, I knew exactly when I hit $1,000,000 in total assets, so I popped another cork, celebrated another great win, and set myself a new goal.

Investing has become a game for me. Some people like shoe shopping, but I like shopping for company shares, ETFs, and other investments. I want my money to make money. I admit it: I don't want to work. I want my money to work for me. Start thinking like the people with money; you will soon be one of them.

To-Dos for Week Twenty-Eight:

1. Find an investment platform. While I cannot give you financial advice, I can tell you that I use Pearler.
2. Invest consistently by automating your investments.
3. Seek financial advice from a professional.
4. Educate yourself about investments by reading. I like *Money Magazine*.

End of Week Twenty-Eight Review

Congratulations. You are beginning to think and act like a millionaire by making your money work for you. You are becoming an owner rather than a worker. You don't become a millionaire and then start thinking and acting like one. You start thinking and acting like a millionaire long before becoming one. Thought and action come first.

WEEK TWENTY-NINE: CREATING PASSIVE INCOME

Passive income, money you don't have to exchange your time for, can come from many different sources. In this section, my purpose is not to cover every conceivable possibility but to give you the overall concept of having your money make you money, not just for retirement but to live on right now. Not only can our investments make money, but we can also create other streams of passive income.

We are trained from birth to get a job and work hard, and then one day, we will have money, can retire, and maybe travel. That doesn't sound very exciting to me. You end up trading your hours for money for the rest of your life, only having enough money to retire when you are too old to enjoy it.

Don't get me wrong. Meaningful work is important, but how many of us have it? Would you continue to work if you didn't get paid? Do you love your job? Are you excited to get up and go to work every day? Working can be great, but working for money? Not so much. Work for knowledge and experience. Work for passion and purpose.

Here are four ideas to make passive income:
- Money from investments in shares and EFTs

While investing and saving for your future, some shares make money in the form of dividends. I buy some shares because they appreciate but pay little in dividends. Other shares may appreciate less in value but pay good dividends. To decide where to put your money to earn dividends, do your research and seek professional advice. Most dividends are paid quarterly.

- Rental income

You can invest in property and rent it out. Even if you break even, someone else is now covering your mortgage, and you are building wealth as the property increases in value over time. But for money right now, you need rental income that is higher than your expenses.

- Money from intellectual property that you create once and then continue to sell

Write a book, design an app, or create other digital assets you can sell and then continue earning money for a long time. I have written several books and got royalties from these works long after they were written. Don't have a publisher? No problem. You can self-publish on digital platforms easily. I use Apple (iTunes Direct) and Amazon (Kindle).

- Have a business that someone else works in, not you

There are businesses you can get into where someone other than you does the work but you still make money. It takes some capital to get into some of them, but they are a good option once you have the money. Have a look at the books and videos by Codie Sanchez for some ideas. *Main Street Millionaire: How to Make Extraordinary Wealth Buying Ordinary Businesses is a good start.*[17] Codie has some great ideas on how to get into these businesses with little to no money if you know how to structure a business deal. Remember, there is a difference between buying a business and buying a job. If the business cannot afford to pay you as an owner, and you must work there daily, you bought yourself a job.

Mind Your Own Business

The goal is to replace your hourly wage type work. When you are trading your hours for money working for someone else, you are minding their business. When making money from investments, real estate, intellectual property, or your business, you are minding your own business. Read *Rich Dad Poor Dad* by Robert T. Kiyosaki.[18] Stop working your butt off to make other people money and start making money for yourself.

You don't quit your day job to do this. You start minding your own business while still working for someone else. Hopefully, you are working at a job that will increase your ability to make money. For example, if I wanted to make money in real estate, I would get a job with a real estate agent, even if I was the receptionist. Then, I would ask questions and learn, learn, learn.

I did a combination of the above. While still working, I started a business. Around the same time, I started working on my first book. I also bought real estate and finally started investing in ETFs that increased in value and paid me dividends. With the several income flows I have created, I do not have to go to work to get paid any more. I still work, but for myself, writing because I love it. I don't have to do it; I want to do it. There is a big difference.

To-Dos for Week Twenty-Nine:

1. Read *Rich Dad Poor Dad* by Robert T. Kiyosaki.
2. Investigate sources of passive income that are available to you. These could be real estate, dividend-paying shares, and ETFs, or you could write a book or develop an app.
3. Measure your monthly passive income. What gets measured matters, and you will be more motivated if you can see your progress.
4. Have a goal to increase the amount of passive income month after month.

End of Week Twenty-Nine Review

Creating passive income continues you down the road of the rich, owners of the world rather than the poor workers of the world. It is a mindset more than anything else. Start small and build. You should also read *Think and Grow Rich* by Napoleon Hill.[19]

The hardest thing to do is to start. You can make excuses not to do this: It's too hard, or it will take too long. If it were an easy get-rich-quick scheme, everyone would be doing it. But it's not, so few try. Be one of those people who do it. The rewards will be amazing.

WEEK THIRTY: MEDITATION

We have done a lot of heavy lifting over the past few weeks, and the steps will be ongoing for some time to come or for the rest of your life. It is time to have a week where we change things up and head in a different direction.

One of the habits of the most successful people in the world is to meditate daily. I once read that you should meditate for thirty minutes every day, except if you are really busy and don't have thirty minutes available daily. Then, it would be best to meditate for an hour daily. Meditation helps you gain a sense of balance. You calm down and enter a state of peace, which benefits your physical and mental well-being.

Take some time every day to meditate. Find a quiet space and relax. Don't try to empty your mind. That is not relaxing but rather putting effort into doing something. It will eventually come naturally. Instead, think of three things you are grateful for.

I like to sit in my living room. It's a lovely sunny spot in my home, and as I live alone, it is quiet. I breathe deeply and close my eyes. I relax my entire body, one part at a time, starting at the top and working down. This takes a few minutes and helps me get into the zone of calm, meditative reflection. I then add to this my gratitude practice and run through three things I am grateful for. We will talk more about this later. What I am thankful for changes on a day-to-day basis. I admit that my children and grandchildren and my close relationship with them often come up. Other times, it might be a beautiful rose I picked out of the garden that day. Or it might be the rain filling my water tanks. They can be big things or small things. I think about them and appreciate what I have. In those thirty minutes, I am not worrying about work, the ironing pile, bills coming up, or the world's suffering. I am just there, being grateful for what I have right now. There is no yesterday; there is no tomorrow. There is just now.

To-Dos for Week Thirty:

1. Pick a time of day you are going to meditate and add it to your daily schedule.
2. Pick a spot where you will meditate, away from distractions, and make it your own. Add a rug, a pillow, a candle, or incense—whatever makes you want to use the space.
3. Meditate for thirty minutes a day.

End of Week Thirty Review

Congratulations. After all the hard work you have been doing, you needed to recharge yourself this week. You have joined the ranks of meditators like Hugh Jackman, Bill Gates, Ray Dalio, and many more. If they have time to prioritise meditation, you do too.

WEEK THIRTY-ONE: BE IN THE NOW THROUGH MINDFULNESS

Mindfulness has become fashionable in recent years, but it is by no means a new idea. It is thousands of years old and incredibly powerful. You probably know from this book that I am very busy and get a lot done. But these two things are different. You can be very busy and not get a lot done.

I used to be very busy, working, having a family life, studying… The list went on and on. I was proud that I could multitask and juggle many things while still getting through the day. I was always trying to get where I was going. Finish that degree, write that book, buy that house. I knew I would finally have made it once I achieved these things. But no matter what, there was always more to do. I was not living for today. I was living for some future date, and I was not happy or very productive; I was just busy.

At other times, I worried about the past. I replayed conversations in my head and tried to work out how to answer that question better or respond to a situation differently. I spent time regretting what I had done or not done and said in the past. This is all a waste of time.

Constantly thinking about negative events or emotions in the past can be detrimental to your mental well-being.

Now is the only time you have. The past is gone, and there is nothing you can do to change it. The future has not happened yet, and you can only affect the future by what you do now. Now is all you have. So, stop living in the past or the future and start living in the now. You have made your long-term plans and set out your goals already. You have created a vision board. Great. Now that these things are done, you can focus on what you can do now.

Another way to look at this is to do what you are doing while you are doing it. Don't worry about the past or the future while doing something today. Just do that thing and enjoy today. For example, each evening, I write a list of what I need to get done the following day. It is a part of my journaling process. Then, on the day I work on that list, I can focus on what needs to be done and just be. Today, I had on my list to make bread. So, when making bread, I was focused only on that and enjoying it. I was not thinking about the past or the future. I was making bread.

Imagine spending your life stressed out and worrying about the future. It hasn't happened yet, and what you worry about may never happen. This is called anticipatory anxiety, and it is harmful to you. Worrying never fixes anything. Worrying does not stop bad things from happening. Worrying is a waste of time and can make you ill.

It sounds so simple, but it is more difficult than you think. It takes a mind shift from where you are to where you want to be. It is work, but it is life-changing. Read Eckhart Tolle's book *The Power of Now, A Guide to Spiritual Enlightenment*.[20] This book changed my life, and I highly recommend it. It will help you start living in the present, increase your enjoyment of life, and make you more productive in moving towards your goals.

To-Dos for Week Thirty-One:

1. Read *The Power of Now, A Guide to Spiritual Enlightenment*, by Eckhart Tolle.
2. Every time you find yourself in the past, stop and bring yourself back to the now.
3. If you are worrying about the future, focus on now. What are you doing right now? Just do that and focus on it.

End of Week Thirty-One Review

This might sound like an easy week, but as you go through the exercise of being in the now, you will find yourself slipping back into the past or worrying about the future. Just keep working on it. It will become a new way of living—a better way of living. Today is all you have. Live it. Love it.

WEEK THIRTY-TWO: CONNECT WITH NATURE

Connecting with nature is essential to physical and mental well-being. People who spend time in natural environments tend to have lower levels of stress, anxiety, and depression. I am blessed to live in a rural area on twelve acres, but that was not always the case. Most of us live in urban environments, making connecting with nature more complex. This connection with nature is as old as the history of man, and our super urban environments are a new reality that we need to contend with while maintaining our necessary connection with our natural environment.

Urban planning now includes green spaces, parks, and places where people can walk, ride bikes, play, and be peacefully at home with nature. No matter where you live, you should regularly reconnect with your natural environment. I do this every week, usually on a Sunday. I walk around my property, down the dirt road at the end of my street, or I go for a bush walk at another location. No matter where you are, city or suburbia, there will be a park you can get to. I make a point when walking to touch the trees, the leaves, the rocks. I want that connection. You might live on the coast and take a beach walk. Let your feet sink into the sand. Paddle in the ocean.

I am so serious about maintaining this connection that I added it to my weekly schedule. Even living in the country, I can let this slip if I do not consciously try to keep my connections strong. It is cold in winter where I live, so it would be easy to stay inside. But it is on my schedule, so I get out there. Once I am out, I love it. This connection is visceral and more important than you know.

To-Dos for Week Thirty-Two:

1. Set aside a time on your weekly schedule to connect with nature.
2. Find and pick one or more activities you can do every week to connect with nature.
3. Do this activity at least once a week.

End of Week Thirty-Two Review

This week, we have added another item to your weekly schedule. Don't worry if you miss a week here and there. As time passes, you will improve at keeping your agreements with yourself. This reconnection with nature will enhance your physical and mental well-being and become essential to your success plan.

WEEK THIRTY-THREE: CREATE YOUR PERSONAL BRAND (REPUTATION IN THE DIGITAL AGE)

Successful people manage their personal brand. It is intentionally created and is how you want people to see you. It can include what you stand for and your identity. Everyone has a personal brand, just like a company does; it is how people see you, good or bad. It used to be based on face-to-face interactions with others, but today, it also includes your interactions on social media. It is the information people use to make judgments about you.

Unsuccessful people also have a personal brand. However, it is unintentional and could be a mess. Those inappropriate posts on Facebook may have been why you did not get the job you interviewed for. Yes, employers check your Facebook, Instagram, Twitter (X), TikTok, etc, these days. How many times have we seen a politician get in trouble over a racist or sexist post they made years ago?

You need to determine your personal brand and then take active steps to create it. Ask yourself, How do I want the world to see me? If you want the world to see you as a successful, healthy personal trainer who can help people achieve their health goals, it is probably not a good idea to smoke or post photos on social media of your sloppy drunkenness at a bar. Smoking and drinking excessive amounts of alcohol do not align with the personal brand you want.

The first step is to determine your personal brand. This would include what you stand for, what you believe in, what you are passionate about, what you do, etc. They should all align. Let's pick someone we might all know and work out their personal brand details.

Jamie Oliver.

What do you know about him? He is a celebrity chef who has written books and appeared on TV shows. Quite a few chefs have done the same but have a different personal brand. Jamie Oliver is very different from Gordon Ramsay, for example. They have a different brand.

Jamie Oliver cares about simple, healthy food. He is especially concerned about children's healthy eating. He wants to make good food accessible to everyone and on a budget. He created Jamie Oliver's Ministry of Food, which has a mission statement: "At the Ministry of Food, we have a big ambition to reach even more people with the transformative power of cooking. By 2030 we want to reach 1 million people through our campaigns—that's 3 mission meals revolutionised."[21] He went to schools and did the school lunches program.[22]

Gordon Ramsey.

Gordon Ramsay, on the other hand, is known for his "fiery temper, aggressive behaviour, strict demeanour, and frequent use of profanity, while making blunt, critical, and controversial comments, including insults and sardonic wisecracks about contestants and their cooking abilities." [23]

Oliver and Ramsay do the same thing: cook, create TV shows, and write cookbooks, but they have very different personal brands.

Work out your personal brand. I did this by creating a vision board for my brand. What did I want people to know about me? Who am I, what do I stand for, what do I do?

So here goes mine. I want to help people live happy, healthy, meaningful lives. Let's live sustainably and within our means. I like a simple life full of good friends, good food, and good wine. I want everyone to be financially secure, safe, and happy. I write books, teach classes, and help people achieve a sustainable life.

Things that align with my personal brand are that I live sustainably. I grow my food and make and bake everything from scratch. I wear simple clothing made from natural fibres. I am usually in an apron. I live within my means and have gained financial freedom through living sustainably. I am healthy due to my lifestyle. I try not to collect too much stuff and live without clutter.

Smoking, getting drunk, overeating, spending more than I make, using credit cards to fund my lifestyle, constantly shopping for things I don't need, and getting into debt do not align with my personal brand.

My idea of a good time is not out clubbing, drinking, or spending a day at the mall shopping. My idea of a good time is having friends over for a good meal, bush walking, travelling to new places, and helping others. If I was given $300 to spend and given a choice between us going out to a fancy restaurant for dinner or going indoor skydiving, you had better suit up and put your helmet on because we are not going to dinner. By the way, it was fantastic. What a rush.

What you post on social media directly affects your personal brand. Think before you post. It will be there forever and may come back to bite you later. Never put your personal business out there for the world to see; it's personal business. Make everything you do aligned with who you are and who you want the world to see you as. I am not asking you to be fake. I want you to work out who you are and be that person. If something doesn't align with your brand, ask yourself if it is something you should be doing, having, or being. Knowing your brand, who you are and who you want to be will help you stay true to yourself. It shouldn't make you into someone you are not.

To-Dos for Week Thirty-Three:

1. Sit down with pen and paper—your journal would be a good idea—and work out who you are. What is your personal brand?
2. Use a vision board to help you create your personal brand.
3. Go through your social media and remove items that conflict with that brand. This will not erase any damage done but may limit it.
4. Consciously create and manage your brand with what you do, say, and have.
5. If you have a negative brand, recreate yourself, starting today.

End of Week Thirty-Three Review

This week's activity will be ongoing for the rest of your life. A positive personal brand will help you in many areas of your life, including getting that job, getting a new client, getting a raise, or getting a home loan. People always judge you when they see you, see a post on social media, or have any other contact with you. It is human nature to judge, which is necessary for survival. Having a personal brand is about putting your best foot forward, always being aware, and having people see you for who you are and want to be.

WEEK THIRTY-FOUR: CLOTHING

Clothing is one of the three traditional basic needs, which includes food, clothing, and shelter. But clothing is more than just a basic need. It is also a way we express ourselves. How people dress can be used to determine their social position, occupation, age, gender, and more. There are dress codes for different cultures, and within those cultures, there are many dress codes for various situations. For example, in Western culture, the only one I am very familiar with, there are dress codes for different events and situations.

You could be invited to an event with a black-tie dress code. That means men must wear a tuxedo, crisp white shirt, and black bow tie. Women are expected to wear a floor-length evening gown. Another dress code is formal. In this case, men wear a suit and tie, and women wear evening wear that could be floor-length, but a cocktail dress would also be appropriate. You can wear casual clothes for a BBQ but not to a corporate office.

What you wear and, therefore, what you have in your closet needs to be appropriate to the situation, and, in addition, it needs to be you. Wearing the wrong thing at the wrong time can adversely affect your personal brand, so it is essential to get it right. It is so important that you could hire a personal stylist to help you determine what is best for you in various situations. You need clothing that expresses your individual style and suits your body shape.

I highly recommend the book *Dress for Success* by John T. Molloy.[24] Originally published in the 1970s, it was updated and revised in 1996. While it is a bit old, the information and good style seem timeless.

While you need clothing for various situations, this does not mean you have to be a clothes horse and have loads of clothes. You need to be thoughtful about your purchases so your clothing does not drain you financially. You want to avoid ending up with a closet full of clothes but nothing to wear, an all-too-common problem.

The fashion industry is there to make money. It wants your money out of your pocket and into their pocket. To do this, they create fashion trends. Different colours are used every year or season, and there are various styles, lengths of dresses, wide-legged or skinny jeans, prints or solids. To see this in action, pick up a magazine and start flipping through it. You will see articles about what you must wear that year or season to be fashionable.

Don't fall into the fashion trap. You don't see classy people wearing the twelve-month best-before-date fashion. This type of fashion will look dated next year. It is also usually made to last about twelve months and becomes washed out or misshapen quickly. Avoid fast fashion. It's a waste of money. According to an article from *The Roundup*, "as much as 92 million tons of clothing ends up in landfills" every year.[25] Much of this fast fashion is also produced in an unethical manner, using child labour or women paid so little that it is hard for them to survive. Sweatshops are, unfortunately, not a thing of the past.

Here are my rules for purchasing clothing:

- Buy classic pieces.
- Don't follow fashion trends.
- Buy the best quality you can afford.
- Good fit is essential. Consider your body shape.
- Go for natural fibres wherever possible.
- Make sure the colour suits you. (Get your colours done.)
- Create a capsule wardrobe.

Classic clothing does not go out of fashion. Its' looks are timeless, simple, and elegant. Because it never goes out of fashion, you are automatically not following fashion trends. Classic pieces are usually more expensive but last longer and can be worn for years. I have twenty-year-old pieces in my wardrobe that still look great. Classic pieces are typically made from good-quality, natural fibres like wool, cotton, and linen. Neutral colours like black, white, navy, and beige never go out of fashion and can become the backbone of a good wardrobe. Pops of colours that suit you can be added to these basics.

For example, the little black dress is a classic, timeless item. Think Audrey Hepburn in *Breakfast at Tiffany's*. It is said that every woman should have one. Why? Because it is so versatile. You can wear it with a jacket to the office during the day or a silk scarf and some jewellery in the evening. By following the first six rules, you can create a capsule wardrobe. A capsule wardrobe is a collection of carefully chosen, classic pieces that are easily interchangeable. The idea is to maximise the number of outfits you can create with fewer good-quality pieces.

Making your mind up every day about what to wear can be painful. You get up and look in the wardrobe at the mountains of clothes you have and think, I have nothing to wear. But if you reduce what you already have to those classic pieces you like to wear, you can add more classic pieces and end up with clothes that make you look good rather than clothes that make someone else in a magazine look good. If you don't love it, lose it.

One way to get started is to cull what you have by sitting down and drawing up a clothing plan. How many shirts should you have? How many dresses, pants, and jeans?

My plan is based on doing laundry once a week, but I keep in mind the seasons.

For warm-weather clothing, I have:

- Three summer dresses for those hot days, all linen and good quality
- Seven short-sleeved summer shirts that go with my pants and skirts
- A lightweight pair of jeans, one pair of linen pants, and a black lightweight pair
- Three lightweight skirts

For cool-weather clothing, I have:

- A warm dress for winter (I tend to wear pants more in the cold)

- Seven long-sleeved shirts for winter that go with my skirts and pants
- A winter pair of black pants and two pairs of winter jeans
- Two winter skirts, one black and one brown

I love to knit and have several warm, woollen, hand-knit jumpers and cardigans. I also have leggings to wear under skirts in winter. They are all black bamboo and of good quality. My one weakness when it comes to clothes is scarves. I love them and have too many.

Finally, a note on socks and underwear. If they are well past their best before date, throw them out and get new ones. Don't keep socks with holes in the toes. They take up space, and you don't want to wear them anyway. As for underwear, if you would not be caught dead in them, throw them away. I am sure we all have those undies in the draw that are so old they are now not fit for purpose. They are stretched out and baggy. Go through your underwear drawer and get rid of anything that you would not want a lover to see you in. That's right, get rid of the granny knickers and treat yourself like a beautiful woman because that is what you are.

Clothing Colour

I recommend getting a colour analysis done by a consultant, or you can do it yourself or with a friend. We all know that some colours suit us while others don't, but understanding why will help you select the right colour for you from now on. It is not so much about the colour but about the tone of the colour. For example, red can come in many tones but still be considered red.

The colours are divided into four groups: autumn, winter, summer, and spring. What group you will be in will be determined by your hair and eye colour and the tone of your skin. Autumn and spring are warm, while winter and summer are cool.

Wearing the right colours can make you look great, while the wrong colour can make you look washed out.

Determining your colour group involves a three-step process:

1. Determine your undertone, whether warm or cool.
   - Cool tone: Your skin looks cool with a grey, blue, pink, or red undertone. You have blue veins and look good in silver jewellery.
   - Warm tone: Your skin looks warm, with yellow, golden, or earthy undertones. You have green veins and look good in gold jewellery.
2. Determine light versus dark contrast.
   - Light means a low contrast between your hair, eye, and skin colour. Additionally, the colours of your skin, hair, and eyes are light compared to those of your ethnicity.
   - Dark means that there is more contrast between your hair, eyes, and skin colour, and you are darker than others of your ethnicity.
3. Determine your chroma, whether bright or muted.
   - A person with a high chroma is bright.
   - In comparison, a person with a low chroma is softer and more muted in appearance.

WEEK THIRTY-FOUR: CLOTHING

If you want to get into this, get the book *Color Me Beautiful* by Carole Jackson.[26]

I have yellow undertones, so I have a warm tone. I have a low contrast between my skin, eyes, and hair, so I have light contrast. I have a softer look, so my chroma is considered muted. I am an autumn, and some spring colours also work for me. When shopping for clothes, I consider this and avoid colours I know will make me look older and washed out.

The result of all this work should be a smaller collection of good-quality clothes that make you look great while saving you money.

To-Dos for Week Thirty-Four:

1. Write down your clothing plan.
2. Pull everything out of your wardrobe.
3. Separate into warm weather and cold weather.
4. Select your best pieces; only put back what is on your plan and what you love.
5. Get rid of the rest.
6. Do or get your colours done.
7. Shop for what you now need to complete your capsule wardrobe.

End of Week Thirty-Four Review

This was a fun week. Getting rid of clothing that no longer fits or suits your age, personality, colouring, and personal brand can be very liberating. Making a clothing plan and shopping to build a capsule wardrobe is a far different experience than impulse buying fast fashion.

I review my wardrobe once each season. If needed, I replace an old piece with a new one. Some clothes work across seasons. Clothes wear out, get stained, and need to be replaced. Don't fall into the trap of keeping clothes that don't make you happy. You don't need to wear clothes with holes in them or that are stained, or that are too big or too small, or that make you look older than you are. You are terrific, so dress like it.

WEEK THIRTY-FIVE: READING FOR SELF-IMPROVEMENT

Reading is one of the most important things you can do. Have you ever heard the saying "Readers are leaders"? Most successful people will tell you that they read.

I have built reading into my daily schedule because it is one of the most important things I can do to ensure a successful life. I finish my morning walk at 6:00 a.m. and have one and a half hours before breakfast, so that time is set aside for reading. This is not reading pulp fiction but rather educational books. This hour is for my self-improvement, which we will also cover in more detail later. For now, know you have to schedule more time for doing great things for yourself.

To get more than you have right now, you need to become more than you are right now. You do that by learning. I read a book a week. Some books are so good that I reread them every few years. Here is a list of books to get you started:

- *Think and Grow Rich* by Napoleon Hill
- *How to Win Friends and Influence People* by Dale Carnegie
- *The 7 Habits of Highly Effective People* by Stephen Covey

- *The Power of Now* by Eckhart Tolle
- *Rich Dad Poor Dad* by Robert Kiyosaki
- *The Four Agreements* by Don Miguel Ruiz
- *Atomic Habits* by James Clear
- *The Barefoot Investor* by Scott Pape
- *Millionaire Mindset and Habits for Success* by M.A. Myers
- *The Psychology of Money* by Morgan Housel

I have mentioned several other books throughout the earlier steps. You need to learn to grow, and reading is the best way. Reading exposes you to new ideas and ways of looking at things. It is a well-known habit of the wealthy and successful. If I wanted to be a successful business person, I would take the advice of successful business people, not the advice of my mechanic. I ask my mechanic for advice about my car. If I wanted to be rich, I would ask Ray Dalio how he did it. Don't you think I can ask him? I sure can! He wrote a book. So much information is available. You can become a successful investor, get into real estate, or start a business. For anything you ever wanted to know, someone has written a book.

Don't like reading? I love to read, but sitting down with a book is unpleasant for some people. Fortunately, many books are now available in audiobook form. Make the one-hour reading time a time to find a quiet spot to listen and take notes.

How you get the information is less important than ensuring you learn daily. Improve your knowledge base, and you will improve your life. Successful people read. Unsuccessful people do not. When successful people are interviewed and asked about their success and how they achieved it, there is one recurring common answer: They read. Saying you don't want to read is like saying you don't want to succeed. There will always be some exceptions to the rule that someone can come up with, but they are the exceptions. If you want success, then do what the successful do. Read. Read. Read.

If you want to do this without spending any money, you can; library membership and borrowing books are free. There is no excuse not to start right away.

To-Dos for Week Thirty-Five:

1. Get a library membership.
2. Add one hour of reading to your daily schedule.
3. Get reading.

End of Week Thirty-Five Review

This is an easy week that builds upon lots of past work. You might already be a reader doing this. If not, joining a library and getting books and audiobooks couldn't be easier. Everyone in Australia, the UK, the US, Canada, and many other countries has access to free books they can borrow. How amazing is that! There is no excuse not to grow and become an expert in any area you want. Once you realise this, you understand that the limiting factors in your life are self-imposed. That is not to say that your life has not had its challenges, but that you can rise above. What if the difference between being you and being a millionaire was one hour of reading daily? Would you do it?

WEEK THIRTY-SIX: EDUCATION

All professionals engage in continuing education. It helps them keep ahead of our ever-changing world. We also need to do this in our personal lives, regardless of what we do for a living. We need to continue to grow and learn. Once you stop growing and learning, you start shrinking as a person. Nothing ever stays the same. Everything is growing or contracting, which goes for us physically and mentally.

You need to learn all the time, and while reading is a great way to do this, there are also courses you can take that will help you grow as an individual. Even better, there are lots of courses you can do for free to get you started. I pay for courses when needed, but accessing free courses is excellent when you are beginning and don't have the cash to spend.

The first place to look for free courses or events is your local library. Free computer and internet courses are available in most libraries in my area. They also have classes and events about cooking, gardening, healthy living, parenting, and so much more.

Government websites offer free training to eligible people to help get them into the workforce if they are unemployed. Centrelink offers free courses on money management. LinkedIn provides a variety of complimentary classes. RASK Education has a bunch of free courses on finance. In addition to free courses, you can get subsidised courses, and student loans are available if needed.

Knowledge is power, so it is worth investing in your education. Currently, I am learning German on a free app that I downloaded onto my phone. In just fifteen minutes a day, I am learning a new language.

Hopefully, you joined a library last week to access free books. Now, you can check out what free classes and events they have. Don't worry; you don't have to join a library to access their free courses and events. Most do require you to register so they don't overbook.

To-Dos for Week Thirty-Six:

1. Check out your local library for free classes.
2. Go online and locate some free classes you would like to do.
3. Sign up for one free class.
4. Consider other classes you may want to do later. These may or may not be free.

End of Week Thirty-Six Review

It was another easy week, which is good because you have done so much work on yourself over the past few months. Now, you are growing your knowledge and interest base, enriching your already great life.

WEEK THIRTY-SEVEN: HAVING A WILL

Preparing for the future is always a good idea and having a will is part of that. You need to plan for the protection and security of your family for the day you are no longer here. You are going to die; you just don't know when. You need to have a clear will that lays out your wishes. My advice is not to wait. Do it now.

You can do this by hiring a solicitor to do a will for you. It costs a bit, but it might be the right choice, especially if your assets are complicated. You can also go to the Public Trustee for assistance. In Queensland, the Public Trustee offers a free service to assist with creating your will. Or you could download a free will kit. Australian Seniors has a free will kit written in plain English, making the whole process easy to understand. My will consists of three major sections:

- Appointing an executor of my estate
- Splitting my assets between my children
- Making specific special gifts

For example, I have three children, so I selected one to be the executor of my estate. I split my assets between them. I also had a few items I wanted to go specifically to a child. I have a significant book collection that would go to the child who would appreciate it most. I have a daughter who likes to sew and would get my fabric stash. You may have unique pieces of art or jewellery that you want a particular person to have. This would all be on your will.

Once you have a will, you need to make sure your family knows about it and how to access it in the case of your unexpected death. I know this is not a fun subject, but accidents do happen. No one plans to have a car accident or to get COVID. And, after you are dead, it is too late to make your wishes known. Money is a funny thing, and not having a will can cause families to argue over assets. We would all like to think that it would not happen within our families, but it all too often does.

If you get a solicitor to draft your will and hold it for you, make sure your family knows who your solicitor is. If you get a DIY kit and do your will, tell your family where it is so that it can be accessed and your wishes are known. There is no point in having a will if no one knows about it and it is never found.

To-Dos for Week Thirty-Seven:

1. Get a will made by a solicitor, with the assistance of the Public Trustee, or get a will kit and do it yourself.
2. Tell your family how to access your will after you have gone.

End of Week Thirty-Seven Review

While there might not have been much to say about this week's step, it was essential. Legal matters are a part of business and also a part of your life. Neglecting legal matters in life can get you into a lot of trouble, so while it may be unpleasant to consider your death, it is necessary.

WEEK THIRTY-EIGHT: HAVING A FAMILY TRUST

This is the final week in the third quarter of your journey to a beautiful life, and you are on your way to creating that extraordinary life by running your life like a business. Once again, we are going to discuss legal matters. Should you have a Family Trust? I don't know your answer as everyone's situation is different, but you should consider it. You need legal and tax advice to determine whether this is right.

A quick online search led me to the Chamberlains Law Firm website, which states that "a family trust is a type of trust generally established by someone during their lifetime for the benefit of their 'family group'. It is a discretionary trust and can be used to hold assets, run a family business, manage certain investments, and support beneficiaries."[27] It goes on to list the benefits as being:

- Asset protection
- Tax efficiency
- Planning for retirement savings
- Flexibility of investment
- Protecting vulnerable family members

Family Trusts don't cost much to set up but require yearly administration. They need their own tax return every year, and you must report how you distributed funds to the beneficiaries yearly. None of this is hard, but you cannot fail to do these administrative functions.

You need to weigh the effort and cost against the abovementioned benefits. Is it worth it? It was to me, and here are my reasons for that.

- It is easy to pass on my assets to my children.

When my mother passed away, my brother and I accessed her will with no problem. It was a simple split of everything 50/50. My brother and I are very close and have had no disagreements. However, even with a will, there was still paperwork, which took time. You can get a lawyer to do all of this for you, but when we enquired, it would cost thousands of dollars. Lots of people get a lawyer to do this for them because, let's face it, they are in grief and broken-hearted about the loss of a loved one. It's not the best time to be doing lots of paperwork.

It took David and me a year to sort everything out before the money from my mother's estate was finally released. I don't want that to happen to my children, so I have all my assets in a Family Trust with my children and me as the principals or appointers. Upon my death, most of the assets will be seamlessly transitioned, with only a small amount outside the Family Trust to be worked out. This works for me because I am in my home on the family farm, with my daughter and her husband living on the same property and working on that farm. My death will not disrupt their livelihood and home.

- I have protection of my assets.

There may be times that you need protection of your assets. This happened to me, and I discussed some of this at the beginning of this book. Due to my lack of planning, I was sued. This person wanted money and as much as they could get their hands on. My home in the country and my business was in the Family Trust, and at that time, I had myself and one of my daughters as the principals. This meant that 50% of the family assets were protected from the person trying to take them from me. If I had not had this in place, I might well have lost my business and my home, becoming another statistic of women over the age of fifty-five who are in desperate financial trouble. Have a look at *The Forgotten Women Project*.[28] It isn't very comforting.

- I can easily run my business through the Family Trust.

As a self-employed writer and public speaker, the Family Trust is a perfect vehicle for running my business. I can easily separate my personal and business expenses by running my business through the Trust. It is cheaper than forming a Pty Ltd and paying yearly fees to the Australian Securities and Investment Commission.

- I save money on taxes.

I have three adult children to whom I can disburse money through the Family Trust. I am happy to be at a point where I can help my children during those expensive years of having young children and mortgage payments. With the Family Trust, payments to beneficiaries allow you to spread the tax burden to those who may be in a lower tax bracket, usually the child that needs the most assistance, as they are on the lowest income.

When you look into this yourself, you may have other reasons for getting a Family Trust, or you might find it is not advantageous for your situation. The point of this week is not to get a Family Trust but to learn about Family Trusts and decide if one would be good for you. If so, then go ahead and get one. It is a vehicle that can make life easier and save you money, but it must be right for you, and talking to a professional would be my best advice. I discussed this with my accountant and had him set this up for me.

Family Trusts are not for everyone. Some people have family members who would not be good to have as partners in control of their assets. I now have my two daughters and me as principals, and I am no longer in sole control of my assets. The three of us are all equal, and we work together. This is not a concern for me as I am close to my family, and I would have no reason to be concerned. It is sad but true that this is not the case for everyone. What if you gave control to family members who took advantage of you? You may not want to form a Trust like this if you are in doubt. There is an upside, but there is a potential downside for some people.

To-Dos for Week Thirty-Eight:

1. Do some online research into Family Trusts.
2. Talk to your accountant or another professional to see if a Family Trust would benefit you.
3. If, after these two steps, you decide that this is right for you, go ahead and get one set up. Only do this after professional advice.

End of Week Thirty-Eight Review

A Family Trust might not be for you, but it can be very beneficial, and you should consider it an option and make an informed decision. I am not telling you to have a Trust. I am telling you to educate yourself, seek professional advice, and, if appropriate, use this as an additional tool to build wealth.

WEEK THIRTY-NINE: MARRIAGE

The history of marriage is fascinating, and the idea of marriage for love is a relatively new concept. In the past, marriage was considered a social contract, a way to organise society. In *The History of Marriage and Divorce,* author Harry Munsinger writes that marriage authorised "sexual relations and the production of legitimate children, governed financial transactions within the family, and determined how assets, titles, social status, and power were inherited."[29]

Essentially, this was an institution created by men and for the benefit of men. Historically, it has been a religious institution and a secular construction, with governments and religions fighting for control. In either case, the controlling people were men. As its purpose was to control property and manage successions and inheritance, for most of history, it had nothing to do with love.

The idea of marrying for love began gaining prominence in the Western world in the 18th and 19th centuries, particularly with the rise of Romanticism. This movement emphasised emotions, individualism, and the pursuit of personal fulfilment, including in romantic relationships.

By the 20th century, the idea of marrying for love had become more widespread in Western cultures. However, arranged marriages and marriages based on practical considerations still exist in many parts of the world. Today, love is a central factor in marriage and is widely accepted in much of the Western world.

While there has been a complete revolution in the reason for marriage, unfortunately, laws have not kept pace in many countries, including Australia, the United Kingdom, and the US. Laws still consider marriage an economic and property agreement, where the participants lose the right to own their property as individuals.

In the past, when a woman married, all of her property became her husband's property, and she had no rights whatsoever. This, fortunately, has changed. Things are more equal now, but you still lose your property rights, as marriage is still a financial contract. When you enter into a marriage, "your" property becomes "our" property. On the surface, this sounds great, but is it? What if you have worked hard for twenty years and built a substantial investment portfolio? You get married, and it is no longer yours. It now belongs to both of you. That would be OK if everything worked out, but in Australia, it is estimated that 44% of marriages end in divorce, and that does not take into consideration de facto relationships ending that have the same negative financial impact.[30] To put this into perspective, "the largest proportion of couples separating and then divorcing were married for nine years or less."[31]

So, if you are all rosy-eyed about getting married, stop for a moment and think. This may not work out, and if it doesn't, you will have to deal with a messy property settlement, which may or may not be to your advantage and may or may not be fair. This is not romantic, but you must consider legal and financial implications of your marriage decision. It is not like any other kind of partnership. You don't get to make the rules. In Australia, marriage and divorce are under the federal government's control. Federal law, not you, will determine the terms of your agreement, and federal court will decide how much of your assets you get to keep and how much you get to hand over to your previous partner. So, in the end, is it still about money and power?

To complicate things, you can be considered married even when you are not. A de facto relationship is also governed under the same federal laws as married people in Australia.

Remember my story from the beginning of the book? I was dating, then engaged, but never married. We both maintained our own homes and kept our finances separate. Nevertheless, after a seven-year relationship, one in which we did not marry, this man sued me, claiming more than half of my assets. This man was renting a house and had nothing when I met him. He had the same when we broke up. I had a home and money in superannuation when I met him and about the same when we broke up. He got all but $5,000 of my superannuation, leaving me with nothing for retirement after working my whole life to secure my future. For him, this was a fantastic financial outcome. For me, it was devastation.

Don't feel sorry for me. It was my fault for not having a plan. This huge wake-up call got me to make a plan, follow it, and become a millionaire four years later. This is what got me to write this book so I could help others not fall the same way I did, and if they do, they can get back up and have a fantastic life.

So, what can you do to ensure this doesn't happen to you?

- Know the law.

I am in Australia, so marriage and divorce are governed by federal law. Get to know the law. If you get married, or even if you don't and enter a de facto relationship, you are covered by a law you might not even know about. That is like signing an agreement you have never even read. If and when things go wrong, you don't want to be in a position where you say, "I had no idea."

- Discuss finances before you marry.

As marriage is a financial contract, you need to talk about this. You should know the financial position of the person with whom you will enter this contract. Does this person have assets similar to you, much more or less, or are they in debt? Knowing might not change your mind, but finding the truth later might be a disaster.

- Have a pre-marital agreement.

You should have a pre-marital agreement. It provides clarity and transparency. If the relationship does not work out, it can offer you some security and prevent expensive disputes later. The downside is that it is not romantic and may only be binding if done correctly. You will need legal advice on this.

- Don't drift into a de facto relationship.

This one may be controversial, but I will stick with it based on my experience. In Australia, Section 4AA of the Family Law Act of 1975, available through a quick internet search, the court considers:

- "The duration of the relationship (i.e. whether the parties have lived together for a period of 2 years or longer);

- Whether a sexual relationship existed;
- Whether there are any children of the relationship;
- The extent and nature of shared residence;
- The degree of financial dependence between the parties;
- The degree of mutual commitment towards a shared life;
- The reputation and public aspects of the relationship and/or
- Ownership, use and acquisition of the parties' property."[32]

In my case, it was a sexual relationship that lasted more than two years. There were no children, we lived in our own homes, the finances were not shared, and there was no dependence. However, people did consider us a couple, and we were committed for the time we were in a relationship. That was enough for me to have to give him my life savings.

What should I have done? Before the two years came up, I could have talked about our relationship, formed a plan, made a pre-marital agreement, got married, or left if he did not want to get married. Anything would have been better than walking unthinkingly into a financial contract, not of my own making but dictated by the government, which was detrimental to my well-being.

I am not saying not to fall in love and get married. We all risk our hearts when we fall in love, and I genuinely think it is worth taking this risk. Life without love is half a life. But remember, while being broken-hearted is awful, it is far worse to be broken-hearted at the same time as having your life savings taken from you or, worse yet, ending up homeless. Not only do you need to recover from a broken heart, but you also have to fight, sometimes for years, to settle the financial side and spend a small fortune on legal fees. When the love is over, it all comes down to money.

- Don't enter a de facto relationship.

Divorce rates are at an all-time high, so don't think it won't happen to you. The odds are not in your favour. There is a way to try to better your odds. Don't enter into a de facto relationship. The separation/divorce rate for married couples is significantly lower than for de facto couples. So, if you get married, you have a much better chance of having a successful relationship. Why do you need to enter a de facto relationship? If you want to get married, get married. Why do you need a trial run? As I sadly found out, having this trial run does not protect you financially. Don't live together if you are not ready to commit or the other party is not prepared to commit.

But you don't have to live with a person for it to be considered a de facto relationship. It seems to all boil down to whether you had a sexual relationship. It was not so long ago that the expectation to have sex outside of marriage was not the default. The default was that you got married, then had sex, and then had children. Today, it is all over the place with people having sex and children before or without marriage. It is called the sexual revolution, and it all came about because of the pill. The pill can be amazing and wonderful; every woman should have access to this technological breakthrough. However, it was a new technology, and just like any other new technology, it has caused disruptions, particularly to the social structures around relationships and marriage. The pill's possible side effects is another subject I will not go into.

Since the introduction of the pill, rates of single motherhood and abortion have significantly increased. This is interesting as the pill was supposed to give women control over their reproduction. It also changed how people viewed sex outside of marriage, which had previously been a high-risk activity for women but not for men. In her book, *The Case Against the Sexual Revolution*, Louise Perry points out that there are cads and dads. The cads want sexual variety and not a long-term relationship. The dads are stable guys who want a long-term relationship. The hook-up culture favours the cads, not the dads. It is, as a woman, "a sexual culture that sets you up to fail."[33]

While it is hard to opt out of this new sexual culture, if you are interested in a successful long-term relationship, consider not having sex before marriage. According to Louise Perry, "The fact that a man wants to have sex with a woman is not an indication that he wants a relationship with her. Holding off on having sex for at least the first few months is, therefore, a good vetting strategy for several reasons." [34]

After her book was published, in an interview with Chris Williamson, Louise stated that she had initially wanted to say, "Don't have sex before marriage or at least before becoming engaged", but on advice for others, she decided to dial this back.[35]

Getting married rather than getting into a de facto relationship will improve your odds of avoiding divorce.

To-Dos for Week Thirty-Nine:

1. Married, unmarried or de facto, you must know the law. Learn.
2. If you are married without a pre-marital agreement, it is too late to change that now, but if you are not, be sure to get an agreement in place as necessary.

3. If you are in a de facto relationship, make some decisions and have some discussions. Do you want to get married? Don't just drift until you have lost the right to choose.

End of Week Thirty-Nine Review

We are now at the end of week thirty-nine, three-quarters of the way through the year and the fifty-two steps to a fantastic life. We tackled a hot topic this week: marriage. Is it an old and perhaps outdated institution? Marriage is great, but the laws around it must be challenged and brought into the 21st century. Before the 19th century, marriages were mostly arranged with the couple's fathers negotiating a marriage contract. Today, we enter into marriage without contracts, allowing governments to determine our fate. While I don't want to go back to an arranged marriage, I do believe that we should reintroduce the idea of marriage contracts for all marriages, not just those who know about pre-marital agreements. Marriage ends in divorce more often now, and marriages are shorter. It is not uncommon to marry more than once, and there are people, both men and women, who use marriage and divorce to get the money they did not earn or save. You can protect yourself if you have a plan. Educated yourself about marriage and divorce so you can make informed decisions, and if applicable, put in place a pre-marital agreement or marriage contract to protect yourself.

WEEK FORTY: CHILDREN

One of the most important decisions of your life is whether to have children. There is no right or wrong choice here. Statistically, most people do want to have children, but that does not mean that you should feel like you have to have children if you don't want to. The great thing is that since modern contraception, we have a choice. What is important is that you and your life partner agree on whether to have children.

If you already have children and are done having and raising children, then this week is an easy pass for you. However, if you have yet to go down that road, you need to make decisions rather than go with the flow. Ask yourself if you want to have children. Does your partner want to have children? These are big issues, and if you end up with a partner who is not on the same page as you regarding children, then the relationship and your happiness are at significant risk.

If you both don't want kids, then you are OK. End of conversation.

If you both want kids, you have much more to discuss. How many kids do you want? When do you want to have them? Who is going to be the primary caregiver? Don't leave these questions till later. Talk about them before you get pregnant.

I wanted to have children but never discussed how many. I wanted to stay home when they were babies, but I wanted to return to work later. I didn't have a plan, but I was lucky to have the number of children that worked for me. It wasn't planned, just good luck. The return to work and study did not go as smoothly. My then-husband and I did not discuss this, and when I returned to work, my then-husband was a stay-at-home dad working on a book. The kids were at school during the day, and my then-husband would drop them off, pick them up, and be with them in the afternoons after school. But if something went wrong, it would suddenly be my responsibility again. A sick or injured child would be brought to my office and dropped off for me to care for. We didn't have clear agreements in place. We had never talked about who was responsible as the primary carer. Eventually, I felt overwhelmed and responsible for everything: earning money, cooking the meals, and taking care of the house and the kids.

This negatively impacted me and my then-husband. With no clear agreements in place, what was his role in the family? Did we know? Did he feel valued? Was he lost? I think he was, and the marriage eventually broke down. We had no plan about having and raising children, and while it was not the only cause of the divorce, it was a contributing factor.

Everything you do needs a plan and an agreement with the participating people. To do otherwise is just setting you up to fail. Having children is a big responsibility, so plan to succeed, and you will have a much better chance of doing so.

If you are not in a relationship but know you want to have children in the future, you need to plan for this. You need to look for a partner who also wants to have children, someone who would be a good dad or a good mom for your kids. I will assume mostly women are reading this book simply because men don't often read books written by women.[36] When evaluating a partner, ask yourself two questions: Would this man make a good dad for my children? What should I be looking for in a partner if I want children?

From an evolutionary psychology point of view, we are looking for a mate who will give our offspring the greatest chance of survival. For a woman, then, we are looking for a man who can provide and protect. Whether you like it or not, women are the ones who get pregnant and give birth. Women are the ones who breastfeed and, in most cases, are the primary caregivers, at least for the first year. Women are the ones who are incredibly vulnerable and need to be provided for and protected at that time. A competent man who is willing and able to step up is extremely attractive. Even if you are not thinking of children at the time of meeting someone, this ability to protect and provide will be attractive to most women. It's a built-in biological preference.

If you are a man reading this book and you want to have children, you need to be that competent man who can step up and provide and protect. If you are, you will be more attractive to a larger number of women and will have more choices of who you can eventually have children with.

To-Dos for Week Forty:

If you have passed this point in your life and the subject of kids is no longer relevant, take a pass this week. If not,

1. Decide if you want to have children and, if so, how many.
2. Discuss this with your partner.
3. Work out the details (when, how many, who will stay home and for how long).
4. If you do not have a partner, ensure that when selecting a future partner, you do so with your desire for children or lack of desire for children in mind.

End of Week Forty Review

This may have been a nothing week for you as you got a pass, having already had and raised your children. For others, it was a big week. Do you want kids, and if so, how many and with whom? What if you are single and want to have kids? How are you going to achieve that goal? Are there other reasons you don't have kids but want to? There are many life circumstances, but having kids is an important goal for most people. People today are having fewer children than in the past, probably due to the availability of contraception, and some people are opting not to have children at all. There is no one-size-fits-all, but you and your partner must agree on this or risk hurting someone you love.

WEEK FORTY-ONE: DIVORCE HAPPENS

Divorce rates are high, and many people have several marriages in their lives. While the right to get a no-fault divorce is a big step forward for those trapped in a loveless or abusive marriage, it did have some unintended consequences. We need to make sure we plan for this possible eventuality, and I covered this in the section on marriage in week thirty-nine. In this section, I want to talk about the process of divorce. I am not going to give you legal advice. You need to get legal advice from a lawyer. I want you to understand that legal fees relating to divorce can run into the tens of thousands of dollars very quickly.

Once you separate, you could run off to a lawyer and have them handle everything for you at great expense, or you could try to be as prepared as possible, do as much as you can yourself, and save thousands. If your divorce is amicable, you could work with your partner (ex-partner) to get as much information together for the lawyers as possible. They will need detailed financial information, bank account statements, loan statements, and asset valuations such as real estate and other investments. Everything you have together and separately needs to be available to the lawyers so they can help you determine how these assets will be divided between the parties. The better you provide information to your legal representative, the easier her job will be and the less it will cost. Try to work out agreements with your partner for the split of assets.

The above approach is not always possible. Some breakups are far from amicable. Is your ex-partner violent? You would not want to put yourself at risk by trying to work out a settlement with them to make things easier for your lawyer and reduce your bill if it puts you at risk for further violence. But no matter how bad your ex-partner may have been, in Australia, we operate on a system of no-fault divorce. This is good because you can get divorced without proving someone was at fault, but as Paul Clitheroe points out in his book *Money, Marriage and Divorce*, "the current system does have a sting in its tail" and "A settlement won't be based on who is at fault."[37]

For example, say you have been married for twenty years, and the assets were evenly earned. No problem, 50/50 might be the best split. But say in that same case, one of the parties was violent and beat the other regularly. This violence is not considered when it comes to the division of assets. So, you could have to evenly split everything with a violent perpetrator who put you in the hospital. Sting in the tail? I think so.

Each case will be different, but it is true that the less your lawyers have to work on your divorce, the lower the legal fees will be. Get over your anger and hurt. Suck it up and try to work with your ex-partner, if possible and if safe, to reduce your legal fees. Don't try to make things difficult for them to get back at them. You are only hurting yourself. I was once told that holding a grudge is like drinking poison and waiting for the other person to die. I have no idea where it comes from, but it is brilliant.

The whole point is to get you to let go of your anger and hurt and work together to reduce the legal costs of divorce. Katherine Woodward Thomas's great book *Conscious Uncoupling* is worth reading if you are even in this situation.

The other thing you can do is try not to get divorced. If you are having problems, try to work it out. Divorce should be a last resort, not your first thought. Consider how your divorce will affect you, your children, your finances, and your living situation. Don't get divorced because you are angry or out of spite. Based on a 2016 survey by AVVO, about one-third of people who got divorced regretted the decision later.[38] The survey quoted did not include cases involving domestic violence, adultery, or alcoholism. Yes, getting a divorce is much easier nowadays, but don't rush into this. You loved this person once. Can you work it out? Can you go to counselling? I am in no way suggesting that anyone stay in an abusive relationship. If you are in one, run!

To-Dos for Week Forty-One:

If you are not married or getting a divorce, this week is a pass for you. In any case, educating yourself is always beneficial. If this is something that is a part of your life right now, then consider doing the following:

1. Read the book *Conscious Uncoupling*.
2. Can you work it out? Can you go to counselling?

3. Where possible and safe, work with your ex-partner to gather information and reach an agreement, saving your lawyer's time and your money. I can see no reason ever to suggest someone stay in an abusive relationship

End of Week Forty-One Review

It's not a pleasant topic, but it must be addressed to run your life like a business. In a company, you do not make emotional decisions; you make logical business decisions. If you are getting a divorce, you need to behave in a manner that is best for your financial future, not in a manner that will cost you money just because you are pissed off with your ex. The sooner you can settle the financial matters, the sooner you can get on with your life. Think of it as terminating a long-term contract.

WEEK FORTY-TWO: HAVING A SIDE HUSTLE OR STARTING YOUR OWN BUSINESS

Most people have a job, not a business, but having a business has many personal and financial advantages.

Personal benefits include:

- You can decide and set your direction without answering to others, giving you independence and autonomy.
- You gain flexibility by being able to choose your work hours and potentially have a better work-life balance than traditional employment.
- Building something from the ground up can be incredibly satisfying, personally and professionally.
- You can express your creativity and innovation through business ideas and strategies.
- By starting your own business, you can create job opportunities for others, contributing positively to the economy and your community.

- Running a business exposes you to various challenges and situations that can help you learn and grow as a person and a professional.

Financial benefits include:

1. Successful businesses can be highly profitable, allowing you to earn more than you might in a salaried job.
2. You can reduce your taxes:
   - You can deduct ordinary and necessary expenses for running your business. This includes rent, utilities, office supplies, salaries and wages, marketing expenses, and more.
   - If you use a portion of your home exclusively for business purposes, you may be able to deduct related expenses such as mortgage interest, property taxes, utilities, and repairs.
   - **Small businesses can take advantage of various tax incentives, including hiring certain groups of employees (such as** those from economically disadvantaged groups), research and development grants, and tax offsets.
   - You can depreciate the cost of tangible assets (like equipment, vehicles, or property) used in your business over time, which allows you to deduct a portion of the asset's cost each year.

I started my side hustle, Green Living Australia, while working full-time for a big insurance company. While I liked my full-time job because of the great people I got to work with, I did not grow up thinking, "Boy, oh boy, I hope I get to work for an insurance company when I grow up."

I worked Monday through Friday, 8:30 a.m. to 5:00 p.m. I worked in the city, so I took public transportation to work. That meant early mornings and getting home at 6:30 p.m. After dinner, I would work on my business. I started with lids for jars to help people use recycled jars for jam-making. My brother did the website, and I wrote the recipes and preserving instructions. Soon, we added other things I was interested in, like cheese-making, yoghurt-making, and soap-making. I published my first book, *Home Cheese Making in Australia*, in 2015. I continued to write and publish, and as I did so, the product range grew.

I was passionate about sustainable living and food, so creating a business to help others in those areas was a pleasure. For the first couple of years, I didn't make enough money to pull any money out of the business. I reinvested and grew the business. This worked for me because it was a side hustle. I didn't need the money and loved what I was doing, so money was not the goal.

Eventually, the business was doing so well that I had to move it out of my house and into a commercial property I rented. I hired staff, first part-time at first, and then full-time. As it grew, I quit my job and worked in the business full-time. Having my brother, David, as my business partner was great. He had the skills that I didn't, and I had the knowledge that he didn't. It was and is a great partnership. Eventually, we bought the building we had rented, outgrew it, and bought another one, doubling our space.

We did all this without borrowing money, except for the real estate. It grew slowly because we didn't put any more of our own money into it after the first cash infusion of a few hundred dollars. We just took the money from the sales, bought more stock, and covered the expenses.

Expenses were low as we ran the business out of my house. And as we went, we learned. We made mistakes but with little potential loss.

So here is my advice on starting a side hustle.

- Don't quit your day job.
- Don't start pulling money out of your side hustle too soon. Reinvest and grow your business.
- Make it something you love to do.
- Have a website.

After about two years, I created a self-supporting business that needed no further investment, and I had an employee so I didn't have to do all the work. And, it could now pay me. Still, David and I decided not to pull money out but took that money, moved into the commercial premises, and grew faster. We had the business for six years before I could quit my full-time job. Green Living Australia was now thriving, and I could work and get paid for what I loved doing. While doing this, I created valuable assets I could later sell. I had real estate worth $1.2 million and about $250,000 in inventory, not to mention the value of the business concept, intellectual property, and goodwill.

So, once Green Living Australia became a successful business, I started another side hustle. I started writing more, publishing more titles, and public speaking as a separate business again from Green Living Australia. That allows me to sell Green Living Australia if and when I want to, but it keeps me doing what I love—writing and speaking.

What can you do as a side hustle? This is limited only by your imagination and your passion.

WEEK FORTY-TWO: HAVING A SIDE HUSTLE OR STARTING YOUR OWN BUSINESS

You could start making something to sell online and at weekend markets like:

- Hand-crafted soaps
- Jewellery
- Greeting cards
- Art
- Clothing
- Cosmetics and skin care products
- Food items (some food licencing may be required)
- Seedlings (very low-cost outlay)
- Wooden toys

Go to some weekend markets and see what others are doing.

You could teach classes on something you are good at. You can market yourself on several websites for free, only paying a commission when you make a sale and deliver the class. I use Humanitix. Classes you could teach might include:

- Art
- Crafting (knitting, crocheting, macramé, etc)
- Sewing or pattern drafting
- Photography
- Calligraphy
- Gardening
- Beekeeping
- Cooking

- Soap-making
- Cosmetic-making
- Fitness and health
- Another language
- Music lessons (such as piano or the cello)

What are your hobbies? Do you want to share them with others and get paid to do so? What are you good at?

You could do odd jobs for others, such as:

- Mowing lawns
- Gardening
- Home maintenance small jobs
- Cleaning
- Child care or babysitting
- Bookkeeping
- Web design
- Social media management

What if you have no special skills to make anything to sell, no special skills to teach or perform for someone? You need to upskill yourself. You can take a class, learn online via YouTube, or get books from the library. We live in the information age; all you need to know is just a click away. Put what you learned in weeks thirty-five and thirty-six to good use.

What if you don't have a job right now? You can't have a side hustle if you don't have a main hustle, but you can still start a business. Perhaps you are at home, unemployed, living on unemployment benefits of some kind. It's enough to get by but not enough to live, save for the future, and create an extraordinary life. No problem. You can go from unemployed to self-employed using the same strategies.

If you are unemployed, you have more time but less money to make it happen. There is lots of free training available for unemployed people to help them get back into the workforce. Take advantage of that. There are grants available to help people get back to work. The worst thing you can do is nothing. Don't think you don't have a choice. Doing nothing is a choice.

Even if you had no financial resources, you could get some seeds and some seed-raising mix for about $20 and start seedlings to sell. How much would you make? Probably not much, and it may get you less than minimum wage by the time you grow the seedlings and spend the time at a market to sell them, but hey, you have to start somewhere. It goes something like this:

- Spend $20 on seeds and seed-raising mix.
- Spend $25 on a market fee. (That is the cost of several markets I have attended.)
- Your total expense would be $45.
- Get fifty seedlings and sell them for $2 each and make $100, earning a profit of $55.
- But you spent six hours at the market to make that, so less than $10 per hour. The money is not the point. The point is that you now have $55 to invest back into your business. You got out there, learned skills, made connections, and built confidence.

People look at me now and say, "You are so lucky to have a business that you love doing, makes you money, and that has set you up for the future." It had nothing to do with luck. I made a plan and worked on that plan. I was growing the business even if I only made enough money to cover my costs or worked for only $10 an hour. I was also learning and growing myself. You can do this.

To-Dos for Week Forty-Two:

1. Research what you can do as a side hustle.
2. Decide how much you can invest to start this, even if it is only $20.
3. Once you have picked your side hustle, get started, no matter how small.
4. Reinvest the income back into your hustle and grow it without debt.

End of Week Forty-Two Review

Starting a side hustle can be fun, but if it's not, you might have picked the wrong thing to focus on. This differs from purchasing an already-established business and trying to make a living. It is a side hustle where you can still rely on the income from your existing job. Yes, it is working a full-time job and then coming home and working some more. But what if it was restoring vintage motorcycles, and you loved to do it? Someone once told me to find something I love to do and turn it into my job, and I would never work again. It is so true. I love to write. It's my job, but I don't feel like I work. I feel like I get paid to follow my dreams.

WEEK FORTY-THREE: FIND A MENTOR

If you want to be successful, you need to spend time with and listen to successful people. There is no point in asking an unemployed person how to run a business or someone who has failed and given up how to succeed. If you want to succeed, ask someone who has done it. You can do this by getting a mentor. A mentor is usually someone in your field who is successful. Someone who can share their winning strategies and help you learn and grow.

You must actively look for people in your field who are more successful than you and cultivate a relationship with them. Most successful people are more than willing to share and become mentors. Join professional associations, business groups, investing clubs, or the Chamber of Commerce, and find people to help you. I joined a writer's group and asked questions. I located people in similar businesses who were not in direct competition and would be willing to help me. After meeting and developing a relationship with them, I called them and asked their opinion on things related to my business. I invited people out to coffee or lunch and picked their brains. I would also then see what I could do for them.

If all else fails, you could hire a consultant. It's like having a mentor, but one that you pay. This could be in the business area, or it could be a life coach. Maybe you are OK on the business front but need help with investments, handling stress, managing your personal image, or tapping into your creativity. Paying a consultant can be expensive, so this would be a last resort. Your first port of call should be a mentor that doesn't cost you money.

I hired a consultant when it was required, and it helped me kick my business to the next level. A mentor or consultant can see your business from a different point of view. They are not in the business, so they may see issues more clearly than you can. If your business is stuck or in trouble, or your life is stuck and in trouble, you are a part of the problem, so having an outside point of view can be very informative.

There are always people smarter than you from whom you can learn. There is a saying that if you are the smartest person in the room, you are in the wrong room. You need to change rooms and listen instead of talking.

To-Dos for Week Forty-Three:

1. Join a professional association, business group, or club appropriate to your situation.
2. Get to know successful people.
3. Develop relationships with these people.
4. Ask for advice.

End of Week Forty-Three Review

This one will take some time and be ongoing. You will always be meeting new, successful people you can learn from. Of course, the first step of learning is knowing that you don't know everything and should shut up and listen. If you think you know it all, you will never learn. If you do know it all, you are already one of the most successful people in the world, and it makes me wonder why you are reading this book.

WEEK FORTY-FOUR: PRODUCTIVITY

To be successful, you need to increase your productivity. I am not talking about working the 120-hour weeks Elon Musk is reported to have worked, but I am talking about cutting unproductive time out of your life. Unproductive time is wasted doing things that do not move you towards your goals. That does not mean you have no fun time. Time off, holidays, or hobbies can all be productive, leading to a fuller and happier life. I am talking about dead time.

The best example of dead time is watching TV. According to Nielsen, a global leader in audience measurement, Australians, on average, watch seventy-five hours of TV a month.[39] That is dead time. You will never get it back; it did not make you a better person or move you towards your goals.

Every time I lecture or teach a class, people in the audience tell me that they would love to do what I do or live as I do, but they don't have time. I always ask them if they watch TV, and they almost always say they do, two or three hours every night and more on the weekends. There were outliers, but these were few and far between. So, it is not that they don't have time; they choose to watch TV instead of creating a wonderful life. Ditch the TV, and your life will change. That time can be spent reading, learning, or working on a side hustle. I do not have more time than anyone else. We all get twenty-four hours a day. We all make choices of how we are going to spend this limited resource.

Another thing that saps productivity is a lack of focus: trying to do too many things simultaneously. That multitasking was supposed to be productive, but it wasn't. I think that everyone would agree that Steve Jobs was productive. Every year, he would work with the development team at Apple and ask for their ideas. He would put them all on a whiteboard, and so many great ideas would come from amazingly creative people. Then, once all the ideas were recorded, he would say, "Pick three". Only three. The rest of the meeting would be spent cutting items off the list until there were three great ideas.[40] That's focus. Think back to week fourteen. With three significant, impactful goals, you will have a good chance of meeting them. With thirty, you will be splattered everywhere and achieve very little.

To-Dos for Week Forty-Four:

I only have one thing for you to do this week: Ditch the TV. That does not mean you can't watch something you really want to see. I don't have a TV, but I can catch a movie on my iPad if I want to. It means stop turning on the idiot box every night and wasting hours watching bad sitcoms that were good the first time around.

1. Stop watching TV.
2. If you are serious about success, get rid of the TV.

End of Week Forty-Four Review

This week will be easy for some and hard for others. I don't know anyone who ever got to the end of their life and said, "I wish I had watched more TV." Watching TV has no positives, only negatives, including contributing to brain disorders such as dementia, depression, and Parkinson's disease.[41]

WEEK FORTY-FIVE: SELECT YOUR FRIENDS CAREFULLY

We are social creatures, and the friends in our lives can significantly impact our physical, emotional, and financial well-being. Author and motivational speaker Jim Rohn said we are the average of the five people we spend the most time with.[42] While I will not take this too literally, I can see how it would work. Let's look at a few examples.

Example One:

The five friends you spend most of your time with are old friends from high school. You all work, so the time you spend together is usually on the weekend. They like to play video games, so you typically meet up on a Friday night at one of their homes and play late into the night. Saturday is a whip-out, as you have been playing all night. Don't worry; you get pizza and a beer and are ready for another great night together on Saturday. On Sunday, you get up around noon, do some food shopping and laundry, and are prepared to return to work on Monday.

How is this going for you? You are spending time with your five closest friends. You are having fun. No harm, no foul, right? How different is the following example?

Example Two:

The five friends you spend most of your time with are old friends from high school. You all work, so the time you spend together is usually on the weekend. You are all into competitive sports and are training for a triathlon. This is how you spend most of your weekends. As an athlete, you watch what you eat and drink. You all like to go to the pub on a Saturday night, but not too late, as you are running in the morning. You also enjoy discussions about politics and the economy and share investment tips, helping each other grow their investment portfolio.

How is this going for you? You are spending time with your five closest friends and having fun, but this group seems to be doing better physically, mentally, and financially.

You get to choose who you spend time with. Choose people that will improve your life. That is not to say you can't have friendships with people who like playing video games or eating pizza. Still, looking for friendships that help you grow, get healthier, be wealthier, or be intellectually stimulating would be best.

Let me put this bluntly: Rich people hang around with rich people, and poor people hang around with poor people. Healthy, active people tend to hang around other healthy, active people. Heavy drinkers hang around other heavy drinkers. Recreational drug users hang around other recreational drug users.

I am not saying stop being friends with everyone who is not rich and famous. I am saying that you pick your friends, and they impact your life. A relationship may be toxic if someone in your friend circle brings you down. You do not have to keep people in your life who are causing you harm. You can just let them go. We outgrow people sometimes, and that is OK. You can't change your friends, but you can change who your friends are. Choose to have friends that help you grow into the best version of yourself.

To-Dos for Week Forty-Five:

1. Evaluate your friend circle.
2. If there is someone who is bringing you down, gently move towards letting that person out of your circle.
3. Consciously seek out friendship with people who can help you grow.

End of Week Forty-Five Review

This week is confronting as we look at that friend who says things that hurt us but then says they were joking, or who drinks too much or complains constantly. We have all had them, and we need to let them go. Find friends with similar interests who improve your life. I do this by asking new people I meet what books they read or podcasts they listen to. It opens up a great conversation and lets me know when I am talking to someone who likes to grow and learn. I will have little in common with them if they say they don't read.

This task will take time and will be ongoing as we build a great team around ourselves.

WEEK FORTY-SIX: SOCIAL CREDIT THROUGH HELPING OTHERS

I first came across the idea of social credit in John Seymour's *The New Complete Book of Self-Sufficiency: The Classic Guide for Realists and Dreamers*, where he wrote about living a self-sufficient lifestyle. While he was a great champion of self-sufficiency, and I agree with his point of view, he also understood that no one can do everything alone and that being a member of society was required. There are times when you will need help in life, and to ensure you get that help, you need to give that help.[43] When giving that help, you earn what John calls social credit.

John is talking about the social credit earned by an individual helping another, for which they can expect returned help in the future. For example, say you need someone to help you move some furniture. It's a job that you can't do alone, so you need to ask for help. How much easier is it to ask for help if you have been a helpful person in the past? I am not saying that you only want to help someone for what you can expect in return. You may never need to ask the person you helped for a return favour. However, I think you would agree that people are always willing to help others and even more so if that person is helpful to others.

Some people never do anything for anyone else; consequently, when they need help, it is harder for them to find it. On the other hand, there are people you know you can call and ask for assistance who will always be there for you. Broken down on the side of the road, no problem. They will come and get you. You know who they are. They have loads of social credit. If they needed something, they would get it because we all know they are always there for others. You want to be that person, not the person that never helps anyone. You want to be known for your good deeds. You want to have loads of social credit. You get to earn a valuable asset just by being a decent person.

You don't need to track your good deeds. You are not keeping score here. It is like a law of the universe. It's called reciprocity. It is natural in a social setting to respond positively to a positive action taken by another. I believe the universe is trying to keep balance. Being good to others can tip the balance in your favour when it comes time for you to ask for help. You don't wait for someone to do something for you so you can repay and do something for them. You can pay it forward, a concept from a beautiful novel by Catherine Ryan Hyde.[44] If someone asks for help, or even if they don't ask, offer to help. Be that person others can count on, and you will find that there will always be someone available to help you if you need it.

You can start with small things, like offering to help clean up after a social event or contributing to a morning tea by baking something. I am 157 cm tall and about 68 kg, so I cannot help with heavy lifting or reaching the top shelf in a grocery store, but there are things I can do for people. Need help with a charity event? I can do that. Want to

WEEK FORTY-SIX: SOCIAL CREDIT THROUGH HELPING OTHERS

take up a hem and can't sew? Let me take care of that for you. I might not be big enough to chop wood, but I can help you in the garden.

There are many opportunities to volunteer. Ask at church, local second-hand stores like Lifeline, or the Salvation Army stores. Join the parent teacher association (PCA) at your child's school. Join the State Emergency Service (SES) or the rural fire department. I joined Zonta, an international group that aims to build a better world for women and girls. There is no shortage of ways to help others.

To-Dos for Week Forty-Six:

1. Start helping others who have helped you.
2. Pay it forward and help others or even strangers.
3. Find a group you can volunteer with.

End of Week Forty-Six Review

This is another task that will be ongoing starting now. Always look for ways you can help other people. It makes you feel great, increases your social credit, and makes the world a better place.

WEEK FORTY-SEVEN: SOCIAL SATURDAY

While you are doing a lot in this amazing life you are creating, there needs to be time for a great social life. Take one day a week and make it your social day. For me, it is Saturday. I usually teach a class on Saturday morning, which is a part of my social activity as I get to meet new people with every class I teach. Still, I generally do not work on Saturday afternoons or evenings. This can be my social time. If you work Monday to Friday, Saturday may be a great time to set aside as your "Social Saturday".

We all get so busy making money, grocery shopping, cooking meals, washing clothes, fixing cars, and mowing the lawn—the list goes on. But you need to take a day and stop. Call your friends who have moved away and whom you don't see anymore. Catch up for coffee with someone. Arrange a movie night out or at your home.

We live in a world that seems so connected, with social media a click away and always in our pockets. Yet, in reality, we are far more disconnected than we think. Liking a friend's post on Facebook is not being connected. We all need real connections, face-to-face interactions, hugs, and good times together. We are pack animals. Friends are critical to our well-being, so engage and stay connected.

Do you have a problem in this area? Make a list of your friends and then think about when you last saw them, talked to them, or arranged to get together. You might be surprised to see that there are people you haven't connected with for a long time. Don't wait. Time passes faster than you think. You might think you can always catch up later, but what if you can't? How tragic would it be to lose a friend and regret not catching up when you have the chance?

The grief of losing a friend is hard enough. You don't need the additional emotional damage of regret. Don't regret that you did not spend time with your friends or loved ones when you could. I recently lost a friend that I went to high school with; this was someone who I had met and become friends with fifty years ago. While I was heartbroken to lose her, I was so glad that we had been in contact and arranged to get together with each other and with a few of our other close friends from high school. I had no regrets about not spending time with my friend when I had the chance—these recent good times together made her passing less painful for me. I felt gratitude that she had been a part of my life, for she made it all the richer.

To-Dos for Week Forty-Seven:

1. Select your social day.
2. On your social day, call a friend.
3. Arrange an outing, coffee, lunch, dinner, or a movie.
4. Add your social day to your calendar and make your social life the focus of that day every week.

End of Week Forty-Seven Review

This is a fun and easy week. You have been working hard to get your life on track to be all you want. Don't forget about your friends and having fun. You will not have one if you don't proactively create your social life. If you don't keep in contact with friends, they will all disappear from your life. Being successful is important and great but being successful all on your own without friendship and a social life is an empty victory.

WEEK FORTY-EIGHT: SELF-CARE SUNDAY

Looking back at the previous weeks, you will recall three basic needs: food, clothing, and shelter. These are all part of self-care. You have to take care of these areas to survive and thrive, and some of these items have been covered in earlier weeks to some degree. I have taken these basics and a little self-love and created a self-care Sunday for myself, and I want you to do the same. Depending on your schedule, you may pick another day of the week, but taking one day out of seven to care for yourself is not unrealistic. It is essential. Let's look at them one at a time.

Food: I like going to a fresh food market early on Sunday morning before church and preparing my food for the week in the afternoon. Have a look back at weeks nine and ten.

Clothing: Sunday is the day that I do my laundry. I wash, dry, and put away all my clothing, ready for the new week. This is easy with a washer and a dryer in the house. I can get this done at the same time as my meal prep. In good weather, I like to hang my clothes out in the sunshine to dry. I love the smell and feel of sun-dried garments, and this way is more energy efficient.

I also do any mending that comes up. Taking good care of your clothing means you don't have days with nothing to wear and never pull an item out of the wardrobe with a missing button because you forgot to fix it. It also saves you money if your clothes last longer because you care for them. Looking back at week thirty-four, you should have a capsule wardrobe of good quality clothing, so it pays to take care of them.

Shelter: This is also the day I take care of my home. I clean and do any little maintenance jobs that need to be done, which could also include some gardening. I live alone, so my place doesn't get too messy anyway. I also have a policy during the week of always leaving a room better than I found it, even if it is putting just one thing away, so my cleaning on Sunday is not a big deal.

A little self-love: By the end of the day, I have taken care of my food, clothing, and shelter, and I am all set to have a fantastic and productive week. Now, it is time for a bit of luxury. My favourite thing to do on a Sunday evening is to take a bath, add some bath oil and bubbles, pour myself a wine, and light some candles. There are no distractions, no interruptions, just me time. I might do a facemask.

Then I slip between fresh sheets, probably have a second glass of wine, and sink into the pages of a good book. Not into reading? Try listening to some good music, playing or listening, or even watching a show you want to watch on a streaming service. Whatever it is, it's all about you.

Spiritual care: If a part of your self-care is spiritual like it is for me, and you go to church on Sunday, no problem. Sunday afternoon should be plenty of time to take care of the food, clothing, and shelter, leaving Sunday evening for a little luxury.

Your goal here is to have a whole day where you take care of your needs and then some of that day to take care of your wants. Most people work Monday through Friday. If you then have a social Saturday, you need a self-care Sunday. If you are not a Monday through Friday worker, whether for an employer or yourself, change the days to suit you. The point is that you deserve a day just for you.

I had difficulty getting one chore done on my self-care Sunday: vacuuming. I needed to make a small change to ensure I could get all I needed done. I purchased a robot vacuum. I have no problem using technology to help me live a great life, and this small change made a big difference to my Sundays.

To-Dos for Week Forty-Eight:

1. Select a self-care day that works with your schedule and add it to your calendar.
2. Take care of your food, clothing, and shelter on your self-care day.
3. Give yourself a little luxury on your self-care day.
4. Take care of your spiritual needs.

End of Week Forty-Eight Review

This is one of my favourite weeks. I love self-care Sunday. It gives me a great feeling to get all my food prep done for the coming week, my clothes sorted, and my house clean and tidy. If I go into the new week with all this done, it is way less stressful. Then, I get the late afternoon and evening to lap up some self-love and luxury. I also take care of my spiritual well-being by going to church. Don't let anyone take this day away from you. You can give and give the rest of the week, but you need a day to take care of yourself. It is not selfish to protect this day. It is survival.

WEEK FORTY-NINE: HAVING A GARDEN

Having a garden is part of my life plan. There is something so fundamental about growing plants, trees, flowers, and vegetables. I have a twelve-acre property, so there is a lot of gardening going on at my place. I have also lived on a suburban block in Brisbane and in an apartment in Sydney. No matter where I am, I grow something. Mostly, I grow food plants, something useful. It helps me save money while fulfilling a need to garden.

Look at growing herbs in pots on the balcony if you are in an apartment. You can grow herbs and vegetables on a suburban block and even have a few dwarf fruit trees. You will be surprised how much you can grow in a small space. There are many other benefits to gardening, such as:

- Gardening helps reduce stress.
- Gardening is good for you physically as it gets you active and outside.
- You can grow organic food, avoiding chemicals that are bad for you.
- Fresh food tastes better and is higher in nutrition.

- Gardening saves you money.
- Gardening is fun for kids and can be a great family activity.
- It allows you to share your bounty with others.

If you are already gardening, this is another easy week for you. Just keep on gardening. If not, what you grow will depend on where you live and how much space you have. Starting in pots is great for an apartment dweller or a beginner. If you have the space, set up a raised bed and do something more extensive.

I started out growing herbs in pots. I then moved on to cherry tomatoes and other summer vegetables, such as different varieties of tomatoes, cucumbers, zucchini, and eggplants. Later, I moved into growing in winter, planting broccoli, cauliflower, and cabbages. Because I have pots and raised beds, the work is surprisingly little, and I now grow just about all my food. When I moved to an acreage, I planted fruit trees and olives.

I feel like I live in the Garden of Eden. The more I grow, the lower my food bill and the more I have to share with others. You can even start coordinating with other gardeners on what you grow and swapping food. I have never been good at growing capsicums, but I know someone who is, and I have arranged a swap for the upcoming summer growing season. I have an excess of rhubarb at the moment that I will be giving away to friends and neighbours.

To-Dos for Week Forty-Nine:

1. Buy a pot and some potting soil and plant something (cherry tomatoes, herbs).

2. Get a seed-raising tray, some seed-raising mix, and a packet of seeds and start some seedlings.
3. If you have the space, put in a raised bed.

End of Week Forty-Nine Review

This is another one of my favourite weeks. I'll take any excuse to get another plant. Come to think of it, who needs an excuse? I now grow all kinds of flowers so I can have fresh flowers in the house for free and have a beautiful garden to spend time in. I know some people dislike gardening, but I don't know anyone who dislikes beauty. So, if you can garden with little effort, like in a few pots, it is a great activity that should be a part of a well-rounded life plan. For me, it is an integral part of being food self-sufficient. I would never be able to have a $30 weekly food budget without a vegetable garden.

WEEK FIFTY: HAVING A SUSTAINABLE HOME

Having a home is a necessity. Housing is one of these three big basics: food, clothing, and shelter. One of the worst things that can happen to a person is to become homeless, and it is a big problem in today's society, even in rich countries like Australia. Having a home can be very expensive. You are paying rent or a mortgage. You have power bills, water bills, council rates (taxes), and home maintenance. Having a place to put your head at night and stay safe can take much of your income, but it is vital to your physical and mental well-being.

Depending on which financial expert you listen to, you are told whether your home is an asset or a liability. Let's look at both statements.

- Your home is an asset.
    - Some financial advisors say your home is an asset, and they are not wrong. If you buy a home rather than rent, you pay off your mortgage, not someone else's. Your home increases in value over time, and it can be great to own your own home. Once it is paid off, you have only the cost of maintaining it and the rates. This is great, and in all likelihood, it will continue to increase in value.

- Your home is not an asset.
    - Assets are usually investments that make you money, not cost you money. Your home does not make you money. It costs you money in rates, energy bills, water bills, repairs, and maintenance. You do not get an income for your home; you get somewhere to live. This is also not wrong.

Your home is and isn't an asset. To make your home a better investment, you need to reduce the cost of running it by making it as sustainable as possible. Here is a list of things you can do to make your home more sustainable:

- Use water tanks to collect rainwater and reduce your water bills.
- Ensure you have good insulation to reduce cooling and heating costs.
- Use a solar hot water system.
- Use a solar power system.
- Have herb and vegetable gardens.
- Plant fruit trees.
- Have a reasonable pantry for food storage, which helps you purchase in bulk and better prepare food plans and preps.
- Have a clothesline, and don't use a dryer. If a dryer is needed, have a low-energy heat pump dryer.
- Carefully select low-energy consumption appliances.
- Have a water-saving shower.
- Have curtains to keep heat in or out, depending on the season.

WEEK FIFTY: HAVING A SUSTAINABLE HOME

I live in the country, so that has affected what I do with my home and how I live, but everything I do can be done on a suburban block. This is what I did:

- I have water tanks and a bore (well), so I am water self-sufficient.
- I have a solar power system for my energy usage.
- I put up a clothesline.
- I have a heat pump dryer.
- I have a work-burning heater to keep warm in winter and lots of wood on my property, so I do not have to buy wood.
- I carefully purchased the best energy-rating appliances I could.
- I put up curtains to keep heat in or out.
- I have ample storage to purchase in bulk and save.
- I have a vegetable garden, herb garden, and orchard.
- I built a house that would never need painting.

I pay rates and insurance for my home every year. The only other house-related expense I have is my internet connection. I live here for very little expense. I work from home, so I get a tax write-off on my home office, making my home cost even less.

Working from home is not a new idea. Think about village living of the past. The baker lived at the bakery. The shoe repair man lived where his business was. It was common practice for people to live where they worked and have the property to be as self-sufficient as possible. Your home needs to supply you with what you need to live well and not be a significant drain on your resources. What we are describing here is urban homesteading. Being self-sufficient gives you financial security.

To-Dos for Week Fifty:

1. Look at your budget from week eighteen and see how much you spend on your home (power bills, water, rates, hot water, etc).
2. Make a list of everything you could do to your house to make it more sustainable and self-sufficient.
3. Prioritise this list and start working on it one step at a time

End of Week Fifty Review

A sustainable and self-sufficient home gives you a fantastic sense of security and well-being. I know that no matter what happens, I can get by on very little. I don't have to because I have built a solid financial base, but things happen. I am sure that people living in Ukraine never imagined what would happen to them and having a home that can produce power and water would be pretty good right now. And if nothing happens, and you never need to fall back on minimal funds, so much the better. You now have lots more money to invest in your share portfolio, real estate, or to give to those less fortunate than yourself.

WEEK FIFTY-ONE: TRAVEL

Travel is another important part of my life plan. If you have gotten this far on the journey through a year with me, you know I love my home. That doesn't mean I don't want to travel and see the world. I have lived in and visited England, America, Mexico, New Zealand and Australia. In December 2024 I went to Austria. The Christmas markets are amazing, and I wanted to go when it was likely to snow.

Travel broadens our minds by allowing us to see other cultures, meet new people, eat different foods, and learn new languages.

Travel doesn't have to be overseas, and there is probably plenty to see in your own country, but I do like to do a bit of both national and international travel. Where you travel to and for how long will depend on your situation. Do you have small children? Can you take off during the school year? How much money do you have to spend? I did most of my international travel before I had children. I started in Australia, then went to the US and then to the UK. Back in the US, I had my children; from then on, I travelled more within the US. I have lived in California, Louisiana, Pennsylvania, and Georgia, but I have visited many other states when I lived in the US. After returning to Australia, I travelled to New Zealand and Austria. Both these trips were after my children were no longer at home and they didn't need me.

What is your current situation? Can you afford overseas travel? Do you have small children or a school schedule to consider? Decide if your next travel adventure will be overseas or in your home country. Once you know this, you can start looking at trips that are within your budget and suitable for your current life situation. Planning your next getaway can be great fun. Let's say you live in Australia and only have a little to spend. Your kids are grown so you don't have to consider school holiday times. Here are some options for you for an inexpensive holiday.

- Forget costly hotels. Find a camping ground that rents cabins. I found a two-bedroom cabin at Wallaby Creek Resort for just $160 a night.
- Stay at an Airbnb with friends. Splitting the cost of a larger house can considerably decrease the price per person.
- Camping is always cost-effective, and you might even be able to borrow some, if not all, of the equipment.
- Go camping and rent your camping gear. Just google rent a tent.
- Volunteer to house or pet sit and get a free holiday.
- How about house swapping as another way to get a free holiday?
- Take holidays where you are volunteering for an organisation.

These ideas should get you going; some can even work for international travel. You don't have to spend a fortune, but you do have to be a bit adventurous.

To-Dos for Week Fifty-One:

1. Decide what you can afford to spend on your next holiday.
2. Decide if it is in your home country or overseas.
3. Narrow down the area you wish to travel to and start looking for holiday opportunities in that area within your budget.
4. Secure your holiday. This could involve house sitting, swapping, or sharing a house with friends. It takes some planning, but it can also be fun.

End of Week Fifty-One Review

This is a fun week. I was working my way through these fifty-two weeks myself, but by the time I got here, I had not been on an actual holiday since 2015, and it was 2022. I needed a holiday. The first attempt was an Airbnb shared with friends up the north coast of Queensland. It was a beautiful place, and the cost per person was low as we organised a group. Unfortunately, it didn't work out for me, as I ended up staying home with COVID, looking at the photographs my friends posted. Later that year, I tried again and spent a week at a beach camping spot in New South Wales in a small cabin-type room. It was inexpensive, and I got to spend time with great friends, sightseeing, walking on the beach, and relaxing.

I skipped a holiday in 2023 to save for an overseas trip in 2024, which I have now taken. Even though it was not cheap to fly to Vienna and back, the holiday itself was not expensive because I was volunteering to help refugees while there, reducing my costs but still allowing me to go sightseeing and have fun. You can find loads of these holidays online, and a holiday where you get to help others is my kind of holiday. This can be a great way to see the world, learn new skills, and make a difference in the lives of others.

WEEK FIFTY-TWO: GIVING

In week forty-six, we discussed social credit and paying it forward. While this is a type of giving, there is more that you can do, and if you can, you should. I am talking about donating money to charity. This is not about social credit; I donate anonymously. For that reason, I will not discuss where my charity dollars go. I will, however, give you some ideas.

Financial contributions can significantly impact the lives of those less fortunate than ourselves. It is in our nature to help other people. We are pack animals and are all in this together as a species. You must think about what kind of world you want to live in. I want to live in a world where everyone has a chance. Everyone has enough to eat, a roof over their head, and clothes to wear. Where everyone is free to live the life they choose. So, while I am helping in my local area, at my local church, at a second-hand store, or in another group that assists others, I am also aware of the needs outside my immediate community.

Here are some ideas:

- Sponsor a child through World Vision or another such group.

- Donate to cancer research.
- Donate to the Smith Family to help underprivileged children get an education.
- Donate to Orange Sky to assist the homeless.
- Donate to the Red Cross.
- Donate to a charity that plants trees.
- Help save the rainforest.
- Bequeath money to a charity.

To-Dos for Week Fifty-Two:

1. Find a charity you would like to donate to.
2. Set up an automatic donation through direct deposit, if available, or through your credit card.
3. Add it to your budget.
4. Don't tell anyone.

End of Week Fifty-One Review

I can't stress enough how important giving is. If we all focus on ourselves, our self-improvement, our home, our money, and our life, then we live an empty existence. Can you imagine living in a world where everyone was obsessed with the self? What kind of a world would that be? The most incredible people in history care more about others than themselves: Mother Teresa, Nelson Mandela, Martin Luther King, and Amal Clooney. OK, I am fangirling about Amal Clooney, but you get the point.

All of the work on yourself is necessary, but you must also become a worthwhile addition to the human race. You have to help others, give to others, and make a difference. If the world was not a better place from you being here, you have missed the point.

WHERE TO FROM HERE

Congratulations on doing a whole year with me. If you made it, I want you to look back at this year and see how far you have come. Your life will look very different than it did when you started. But this trip is not over.

This is something you need to do again and again. It will be much easier next time, and the gains will be even more significant, but creating a fantastic life is not a one-shot and done. It takes continual effort for the rest of your life. The more you do this, the better your life gets. These fifty-two steps must be a permanent part of your life, and it takes some effort to keep them all working together.

I could do better, and I know I let things slide occasionally. To keep myself on track, I go back to the beginning of this book as soon as I finish step fifty-two and start again. I keep myself to just one step a week and review that step. Am I still happy with my daily schedule as I set out in week one? When I get to week eight, exercise, I review my exercise plan. Is it still working for me? Do I need to up my game? When I get to week thirty-four, clothing, I pull everything out of the closet and review what I have. What do I need to get rid of? What do I need to replace?

It is so much easier the second time around. The new gains build on last year's gains, making life more remarkable. You make bigger and better goals. You learn more, become more valuable to the community, give more, and feel more. You know you have done it; you have built a fantastic life that will continue to improve from here.

So, this week's to-do list is to go back to the beginning of the book and start again at week one. Oh, and if you did the work, this worked for you. If that is the case, share this with someone else. Play it forward

ABOUT THE AUTHOR

Valerie Pearson is a writer and public speaker interested in simple living, sustainability, and achieving financial freedom through a self-sufficient lifestyle.

In 2004, Valerie co-founded Green Living Australia, located just south of Brisbane in Queensland, Australia. This company provides ingredients, equipment, and education for making cheeses and yoghurt, fermenting, home preserving, soap making and other self-sufficient, sustainable living skills.

Valerie published her first book, *Home Cheese Making in Australia*, in 2015. Her second book, *Sugar-Free Home Preserving*, was published in 2019. In 2021, Valerie published her third book, *Gut Health and Fermented Foods*.

Valerie continues writing and teaching, speaking about healthy living, sustainability, and financial freedom through a self-sufficient lifestyle. Valerie lives in rural Queensland in the Granite Belt region, where she finds the cool, high country perfect for growing herbs and vegetables in her garden and fruit in her orchard, baking sourdough bread, sitting by the fire in winter, and drinking wine with friends.

valeriepearson.com.au.

END NOTES

1. "De Facto Relationships | Federal Circuit and Family Court of Australia." n.d. www.fcfcoa.gov.au. https://www.fcfcoa.gov.au/fl/pubs/defacto.
2. Rohn, Jim. 2005. *How to Use a Journal.* R & L Publishing dba Success Media.
3. Fogg, B.J. 2019. *Tiny Habits: The Small Changes That Change Everything.* Audible Studios.
4. Fogg, B.J., ibid.
5. OZHARVEST. 2024. "Food Waste and Hunger Facts." https://www.ozharvest.org/food-waste-facts/.
6. "Payments Statistics." n.d. Reserve Bank of Australia. https://www.rba.gov.au/payments-and-infrastructure/resources/payments-data.html.
7. Kim, W Chan, and Renée Mauborgne. 2015. *Blue Ocean Strategy: How to Create Uncontested Market Space and Make the Competition Irrelevant.* Boston, Massachusetts: Harvard Business Review Press.
8. Written by Benjamin Franklin to Jean-Baptise LeRoy in a letter written in 1789.
9. Parkinson, Cyril Northcote. 1996. *Parkinson's Law.* Buccaneer Books.
10. A Current Affair. 2024. "Terminally Ill Grandfather Stopped from Accessing His Super Payout Due to Spelling Mistake He Didn't Make." Nine.com.au. February 20, 2024. https://9now.nine.com.au/a-current-affair/terminally-ill-grandfather-stopped-from-accessing-superannuation-pay-out-due-to-tiny-/5b524cec-a1e2-4c13-9720-d1fddd4d17f9.

11. A Current Affair. 2021. "Struggling Mum Battling Cancer Denied from Accessing Her Own Super | a Current Affair." YouTube. September 7, 2021. https://www.youtube.com/watch?v=zPvqfoVKUbQ.
12. Clason, George S. 1955. *The Richest Man in Babylon*. Hawthorne Books. Stanley, Thomas J., and Wiliam D. Danko. 1998.
13. *The Millionaire Next Door: The Surprising Secrets of America's Wealthy*. New York: Pocket Books.
14. Bradney-George, Amy, and Amy Bradney-George. 2011. "Australian Household Debt Statistics." Finder.com.au. finder. May 28, 2011. https://www.finder.com.au/ credit-cards/australias-personal-debt-reported-as-highest-in-the-world#.
15. Smith, Lisa. 2019. "Good Debt vs. Bad Debt: What's the Difference?" Investopedia. 2019. https://www.investopedia.com/articles/pf/12/good-debt-bad-debt.asp.
16. Ibid.
17. Sanchez, Codie. 2024. *Main Street Millionaire: How to Make Extraordinary Wealth Buying Ordinary Businesses*. Penguin Group.
18. Kiyosaki, Robert. 2022. *Rich Dad Poor Dad, What the Rich Teach Their Kids About Money That the Poor and Middle Class Do Not!* 25th edition. Plata Publishing.
19. Hill, Napoleon. 2007. *Think and Grow Rich*. New York: Jeremy P. Tarcher.
20. Tolle, Eckhart. 2000. *The Power of Now: A Guide to Spiritual Enlightenment*. Sydney, NSW: Hodder Headline Australia.
21. "Jamie's Ministry of Food." n.d. Jamie's Ministry of Food. https://www.jamiesministryoffood.com.
22. Wikipedia Contributors. 2021. "Jamie's School Dinners." Wikipedia. Wikimedia Foundation. January 23, 2021. https://en.wikipedia.org/wiki/Jamie%27s_School_Dinners.
23. Wikipedia Contributors. 2019. "Gordon Ramsay." Wikipedia. Wikimedia Foundation. April 19, 2019. https://en.wikipedia.org/wiki/Gordon_Ramsay.
24. Molloy, John T. 1975. *Dress for Success.* New York Peter H. Wyden.

END NOTES

25. Ruiz, Arabella. 2024. "17 Most Worrying Textile Waste Statistics & Facts." TheRoundup.org. TheRoundup. March 18, 2024. https://theroundup.org/textile-waste-statistics/.
26. Jackson, Carole. 1980. *Color Me Beautiful*. Ballantine Books.
27. "Chamberlains." 2024. Chamberlains Law Firm. October 28, 2024. https://chamberlains.com.au.
28. "The Forgotten Women." 2016. The Forgotten Women. 2016. https://www.theforgottenwomen.org.au.
29. Munsinger, Harry L. 2019. *The History of Marriage and Divorce*. Archway Publishing.
30. Greer, Damien. 2023. "Marriage and Divorce Statistics Australia." Damien Greer Lawyers. February 25, 2023. https://damiengreer.com.au/family-law/statistics/marriage-divorce-statistics-australia/.
31. Qu, Lixia, and Jennifer Baxter. 2023. "Divorces in Australia." Australian Institute of Family Studies. March 2023. https://aifs.gov.au/research/facts-and-figures/divorces-australia-2023.
32. "What Is a de Facto Relationship | Claiming de Facto Status." n.d. Damien Greer Lawyers. https://damiengreer.com.au/family-law/de-facto-relationship-australian-law/.
33. Perry, Louise. 2022. *The Case against the Sexual Revolution: A New Guide to Sex in the 21st Century*. John Wiley & Sons.
34. Ibid.
35. Chris Williamson. 2023. "The Terrible Truth about the Sexual Revolution - Louise Perry (4K)." YouTube. December 4, 2023. https://www.youtube.com/watch?v=HAmQ7Tcrh6A.
36. Sieghart, Mary Ann. 2022. *The Authority Gap: Why Women Are Still Taken Less Seriously than Men, and What We Can Do about It*. New York, NY: W. W. Norton & Company.
37. Clitheroe, P. (2003). *Money, Marriage & Divorce*. Penguin Books.
38. AVVO. 2016. "2016 Annual Relationship, Marriage, and Divorce Survey Final Report." 2016. https://marketing-assets.avvo.com/media-resources/avvo-research/2016/avvo_relationship_study_2016_final_report.pdf.

39. Nielsen. 2018. "Screen Time Still an Australian Pastime." March 2018. https://www.nielsen.com/insights/2018/screen-time-still-an-australian-pastime/.
40. Isaacson, Walter. 2011. *Steve Jobs*. New York: Simon & Schuster.
41. Salamon, Maureen. 2024a. "Too Much TV Might Be Bad for Your Brain - Harvard Health." Harvard Health. Harvard Health. March 2024. https://www.health.harvard.edu/mind-and-mood/too-much-tv-might-be-bad-for-your-brain.
42. Rohn, J. 1993. *The Art of Exceptional Living*. Rohn Publications.
43. Seymour, J. 1993. *The New Complete Book of Self-Sufficiency: The Classic Guide for Realists and Dreamers*. DK Publishing.
44. Hyde, C. R. 2000. *Pay It Forward*. Island Books

www.ingramcontent.com/pod-product-compliance
Lightning Source LLC
Chambersburg PA
CBHW051558010526
44118CB00023B/2736